WHY
AMERICA
IS
BANKRUPT

ALSO BY PETER JEDICK

LEAGUE PARK

CLEVELAND: Where the East Coast Meets the Midwest

HIPPIES, a novel

THE WEST TECH TERRORIST, a young adult World War II mystery

WHY AMERICA IS BANKRUPT

Who Did It and How To Fix It

PETER JEDICK

HOOK AND LADDER PRESS
Rocky River, Ohio

CREATESPACE INDEPENDENT PUBLISHING PLATFORM

For information contact:

Peter Jedick

(www.peterjedick.com)

First edition, February, 2016

Cover Design by Denise Ziganti and John Scavnicky
of Design Direction
(www.dezindz.com)

Print layout and eBook editions by eBooks By Barb
for booknook.biz

TABLE OF CONTENTS

PART FOUR: AUTHOR PETER JEDICK'S PUBLISHED ARTICLES

PART ONE:
THE REASON FOR
OUR MASSIVE DEBT

"To contract new debts is not the way to pay old ones."
—George Washington, our nation's first president,
The Father of Our Country, in a letter to James Welch, April 7, 1799.

PREFACE:
WHY I USED TO BE A LIBERAL

CALL ME OLD-FASHIONED but I still like to read the print copy of my daily newspaper, the Cleveland *Plain Dealer*, Ohio's Largest Newspaper. What I like about the print copy is often times when I'm reading one story I stumble across another one of interest. It's hard to do that on a tablet.

Back in 2007 I happened upon a story buried in the back of the paper. It was about a group of students at Oberlin College trying to start a Young Republican club. You might have heard of Oberlin's reputation as one of the most liberal campuses in America so they were underdogs to say the least.

Well, there was a photo with the story that immediately caught my eye. The Young Republicans put up a sign about an organizational meeting and some of our "best and brightest" young students painted swastikas on the sign.

Hopefully, if you are intelligent enough to be reading this book you know that swastikas were the symbol of Adolf Hitler's fascist Nazi Party. They were responsible for killing millions of people who didn't agree with their views before and during World War II.

So these students were trying to equate the Republican Party with fascism. Well, I am a registered Republican voter so I was immediately upset by the reference for a number of reasons.

First of all, my father was a soldier during World War II, the war that put fascism out of business. He parachuted into France on D-Day, a heroic feat that I think about every day.

Can you imagine jumping out of an airplane in the middle of the night, not knowing where you are landing, while carrying a rifle and about one hundred pounds of crap on your back? And then you land in the middle of a cornfield surrounded by enemy soldiers wanting to kill you? What my father did still amazes me to this day. And since this book is a lot about a father's role in our modern society I hope you keep his memory in mind as you read it.

Yet my father did not act alone. Any student of World War II understands that there were thousands of stories just like his. The sacrifices that my dad and his whole generation made to keep the world safe for democracy were huge.

My dad also ended up as a prisoner of war in a German concentration camp. So I also think of him any time the subject of the Holocaust is raised. He did not have it as bad as the Jews under the Nazis but he had little food and warmth during one of Europe's coldest winters on record. The suffering he must have endured every day still tears me up. He returned to America weighing only 90 pounds and with a bad case of post-traumatic stress disorder (PTSD). I wouldn't recommend his weight loss program to anyone.

So when I read that these students were comparing America's Republican Party, the party of Abe Lincoln, to Hitler's Nazi Party, it upset me greatly. I thought to myself, "What are they teaching these kids?" They are in desperate need of a history lesson and I am just the person to give them one.

I called the student who was trying to organize the Young Republicans and offered to visit campus and give a talk titled: "Why I Used to Be a Liberal." And I told him that I did not just want to preach to a bunch of future Republicans who agreed with me. I wanted to meet with the enemy camp as well. I asked him to publicize my speech as an open challenge to all of the students on campus who disagreed with my premise.

Much to my surprise about 50 students showed up on a bitter cold winter's night. In fact, the college did not give me a large enough space and we had standing room only. We had a lively discussion that I enjoyed thoroughly. Here are some highlights I still remember.

First, I asked them all to stand and say the Pledge of Allegiance to the United States of America like we used to do every day when I was in grade school. I could tell it made many of them uncomfortable but they went along with it just to humor me. I was curious what their reaction would be.

Secondly, I told them that I wanted to record the meeting with my video camera for my own personal reference only. I wanted to look back on my performance and see what I could learn from it. But many of the students objected. From what I gathered they felt the Pledge of Allegiance was pushing it but the fear of being seen with a bunch of Republicans was too much for their young psyches.

It could permanently damage their liberal reputations. I thought it was quite strange from my point of view but I acquiesced and turned off my camera. Looking back I wish I was more forceful. I would love to watch it again today. But they did give me a nice write-up in the campus newspaper, *The Oberlin Review*. (You can find a link to the article at my web site: www.peterjedick.com)

So I gave them a quick speech on how I was a lot like them when I was their age. How I came from a family of Democrats in Cleveland where Republicans were branded as the rich people's party and the Democrats represented the working poor like my family.

How when I was in college we hated Republican President Richard Nixon because he represented the Vietnam War, even though it was two Democrat Presidents who put our troops on the ground there, John F. Kennedy and Lyndon B. Johnson. I explained to them how most of us baby boomers were taught to be Democrats and how since most of their professors shared my college pedigree their profs were probably teaching them the same mantra.

But—and here was the big BUT—my views changed as I grew older. I basically gave them the capsule version of this book. I told them their views might change also once they went out into the real world, got a haircut, got a real job, raised a family and paid taxes. And more importantly, once they discovered what the government was doing with their tax money.

Then I added how it was really two of my many jobs that made me not only a Republican, but a dreaded conservative Republican. I told them how as a substitute teacher in the Cleveland public school system I was forced to deal with the school busing experiment, a brainchild of the Democrats. I explained how much it hurt me to witness the destruction of a once great public school system, especially since I was a Cleveland public school graduate myself.

Then I told them a few stories from the Cleveland Fire Department about welfare families and Affirmative Action, two more Democratic darlings that I had been forced to deal with during my career.

After that I opened the floor to questions.

We went back and forth and had a rousing discussion. I enjoyed it thoroughly. The students were intelligent and well educated but they were quite naïve, which is what I expected. It was all going very smoothly until one non-Republican accused me of being a closet racist.

I was a bit taken aback but before I could defend myself one of the new Republicans came to my defense. She was a black student from the Bronx in New York City, the exact opposite of what you would expect to be a Young Republican.

She grew up in one of the Big Apple's huge public housing projects and she told the white kids how all her black girlfriends from high school just wanted to have a baby and go on welfare.

BINGO! I was in heaven. This young girl was talking my language. It was like the parting of the sea. As you will discover throughout this book, my main thesis is that unwed moms receiving loads of free stuff is the biggest threat to our nation's health and future. It is also the reason our inner cities are still wracked with poverty and crime.

Since this defense came out the mouth of a young black woman the white kids had nothing to say in response. They were flabbergasted. The reason the white kids were in shock is that they mostly grew up in sheltered suburban environments where they did not have to deal with the consequences of their liberal beliefs.

I rested my case and invited the students who still wanted to talk to meet me at the local watering hole. Once again I was surprised by how many of them showed up. We closed the joint on a cold winter's evening.

It was all good. I came back to Cleveland with a grateful sense of accomplishment and an idea for a book, this book.

CHAPTER ONE:
THE INTRODUCTION

"Freedom is a fragile thing and is never more than one generation away from extinction"—Ronald Reagan, Inauguration Speech as Governor of California, January 5, 1967

THANKS TO THE Oberlin students I had the idea for this book. But my incentive to write it actually came about when I neared retirement and realized that I had been paying taxes for over half a century. The same goes for all my friends and family members. Yet our nation is bankrupt.

When I started writing this book back in 2014 my goal was to explain why our once rich nation was now overwhelmingly in debt. Trillions upon trillions of dollars in debt. And how dangerous this staggering debt is to our country's defense and its future.

I wanted to explain how our country found itself in this mess and do it in simple terms that any American could understand.

I hoped to point out that this is not a new problem. That it has been going on throughout my entire adult lifetime, stretching over the past 50 years, since the Kennedy/Johnson administrations.

I also wanted to show how many of our federal social programs are the root of all our troubles because they encourage unwed mothers to make babies. And since many of these social programs overwhelmingly benefit our African American population, I needed to tackle the race problems plaguing our society as well.

I wanted to show how most of these programs were actually counterproductive to their intended goals. How they actually created a Black Subculture (BSC) in our society.

Then I was going to show how the BSC affects the fabric of our entire nation in ways that most Americans fail to understand.

I also wanted to explain to my readers the inner workings of many government programs that influence our lives in ways they might not understand. Programs like public housing, school busing, Obamacare, immigration reform, Freddie Mac and Fannie Mae not only cost us a fortune but they put our entire democracy at risk. Put them all together and they are the reason our country is crippled by an ever-increasing mountain of debt.

For example, in my chapter on "Where Our Taxes Go" I will speculate that within my lifetime, while I was paying taxes for 50 years, one unwed black teenage mom could have created 39 government dependents whom never paid a penny in taxes from their cradle to their grave.

How did I come up with such a fantastic figure? Easy, I just did the math. You start with a 16-year-old unwed mom having a baby when I was 16. If she has a couple more babies by the time she is twenty, her three kids can each have three babies themselves, making nine grandkids by the time she is 36. By the time Grandma is 56 she can have 27 great-grand kids, for a grand total of 39 dependents.

I'd like to find someone to figure out the total cost of all those dependents to our nation's economy. No wonder our nation is broke.

Finally, and most importantly, I wanted to offer some radical solutions on how we can erase our crushing debt before it bankrupts the America of our children and grandchildren.

But then an unarmed black youth in Ferguson, Missouri, harassed a white cop and the cop shot and killed him. All hell broke loose across our nation's landscape and suddenly the race question was front and center in all of our conversations.

I keep hearing everyone say that what America needs is an honest conversation about race. But it never happens. Why not? Because white people are too afraid of being called "racist" to honestly address our race problem, especially if their livelihoods could be endangered. And many black leaders do not want to take any of the responsibility for the mess we as a nation find ourselves in.

A white journalist or college professor could see his or her entire career go up in flames just by being accused of using the "N" word as far back as two decades ago. For example, a young female television announcer in my home town of Cleveland, Ohio, recently found herself in a load of trouble for using the term "jigaboo" on the air. She did not know its historic racial connotations that any baby boomer would.

Black journalists and academics face a similar problem. If they in any way imply that maybe the black race should better police itself and its neighborhoods, other black leaders will instantly tag them as an "Uncle Tom." Why risk the chance of ruining your career? Better to just go with the flow and not upset the apple cart.

However, since I am a recently retired white guy I am going to step out on a limb here. I hope my friends and colleagues do not consider me a "racist" when I challenge some of our black leaders about their current views.

I've enjoyed the time I spent with many of the African Americans that I've met during my lifetime. It is the Black Subculture that our government has created that I have a problem with. Surprisingly, there are some black leaders who actually agree with my arguments.

Hopefully, I do not have to worry about losing a source of income if I try to portray our race problems in an honest fashion. I think it would be difficult for President Obama to yank my social security benefits after he reads this book.

I also hope that my friends who still consider themselves members of the Democrat Party will not hold it against me when I take their party to the toolshed for creating our bankrupt nation. Of course, I am not blam ing the average citizen who automatically votes Democrat just like my father did for many years. After all, if not for a few unique career choices, I would probably still be a card-carrying Democrat myself.

This is history, guys, don't take it personal.

My book argues that the Democratic politicians of my generation are primarily responsible for our staggering national debt. Of course, they had some help from across the aisle but all these insane policies can be traced back to when Democratic President John F. Kennedy created a policy called "Deficit Funding." Then Democratic President Lyndon B. Johnson tried to create something called "The Great Society" while at the same time funding the Vietnam War.

There was an old saying that a nation can't buy both "guns and butter." LBJ thought otherwise. We will look at the results of his "Great Society" with a critical eye.

So here is my take on the racial and financial problems of twenty-first century America. Very sadly, our race problems and our debt problems are intricately intertwined.

Do you want to know why there is still rampant racism in the twenty-first century United States of America, 160 years after the Civil War? Very simple. It is because many inner city black families do not have fathers.

Do you want to know why after a 50 year "War on Poverty" there is still widespread poverty in our inner city black communities? Very simple. It is because many inner city black families do not have fathers.

Do you want to know why inner city public schools are largely dysfunctional? Very simple. It is because many inner city black families do not have fathers.

Do you want to know why all the city of Cleveland neighborhoods where I lived and worked are now dangerous, crime-ridden wastelands? Very simple. It is because many inner city black families do not have fathers.

I could go on and on but I think you get the point. The reason for the large number of blacks incarcerated in our prisons? A lack of father figures. The reason unarmed black youths are shot and killed by both black and white cops? Few black male role models in their homes.

So this brings us to the really BIG question, the main thesis of this book.

Why is the United States of America on the verge of bankruptcy and trillions and trillions of dollars in debt? One more time. Because there are not enough black fathers in inner city families.

Why America Is Bankrupt will show you all the connections.

Which brings us to one last final BIG question. Why are there so few fathers in our black inner city families? Because the federal government gives unwed black mothers a plethora of welfare programs so they can create more babies. It all goes back to a program called Aid to Families of Dependent Children (AFDC). It has since been replaced but its mindset still holds sway in the black community. Very simply, if the moms do not have a husband they are qualified for more free stuff.

Who would come up with such a crazy system? Especially one that costs American taxpayers billions upon billions of dollars a year, directly and indirectly. And it is the source of most of our social, domestic and financial problems.

But before we go on to the main text of my book let us step back a minute and take another brief look at our nation's racial problems and try to frame them in a way the average reader can understand them.

After the Ferguson, Missouri, police shooting incident, the issue of black youths being shot by white cops became a huge story with the media. We even had a couple of them in my home town of Cleveland, Ohio.

The shootings sparked riots and protests reminiscent of the 1960s. Black leaders cried discrimination. Local and national newspaper columnists tried to explain the situation. Conservative radio talk show hosts added alternative viewpoints. It seemed for a while that every week there was another shooting and more media hype.

Even President Barack Obama and his Attorney General, Eric Holder, became part of the story, presenting calls for action and starting Federal Justice Department investigations.

All this occurred while I was trying to write a simple book explaining why the United States of America was going bankrupt. It seemed no one was talking about such an important subject, especially with a presidential election on the horizon for 2016.

But all it took was for one poor white cop to shoot one poor black kid and there was suddenly a national debate on many of the subjects that I wanted to write about. It all ties in together: racism, poverty, taxes and bankruptcy.

My utmost hope is that my book will change the conversation about what is wrong with America. We need some major policy shifts in order to survive but our professional politicians and our mainstream media are not even addressing these issues.

In most books the author creates arguments that build toward a conclusion at its end. This book will do just the opposite. In my fourth chapter I will provide the major changes that we need to embrace. For the rest of the book I will lay out the arguments for why we need these changes. I am doing this because many of today's young readers have a very short attention span. If they only read the first four chapters maybe it will spark them to act.

I will support my arguments mainly with examples from my own life. And I will back them up with articles from the two media outlets that I read regularly, the Cleveland *Plain Dealer*, Ohio's Largest Newspaper, and *The Week Magazine* which has replaced *Time* and *Newsweek* as my prime sources of national news. For the past year I have been saving articles that support my views. Every day there is at least one article, often two or more, that fit my theory. Yet even our most educated readers may not know how to interpret them unless they read my book first.

I could easily overwhelm you with facts and figures and tons of documentation. But I am not writing an academic thesis even though I could. Instead I pledge to explain my ideas in a plain straightforward manner. In other words, I will show the reader how to connect the dots, to better understand what is going on right under our noses.

I also intend to raise questions about topics that our media and academia are afraid to investigate for fear of being labeled "racist" or "politically incorrect." It is a sad state of affairs for our once valued universities and newspapers. After discussing many of these topics I will end by stating: "Someone Should Do A Study" or (SSDAS). It is a challenge to my peers in the academic and journalistic communities. However it is one that I doubt they willingly accept.

I know this may all sound a bit overwhelming but please read on, my fellow Americans, as I attempt to make sense of this crazy situation in which all of us twenty-first century Americans find ourselves.

CHAPTER TWO:
ABOUT THE AUTHOR

"I have spent most of my life as a Democrat. I recently have seen fit to follow another course. I believe that the issues confronting us cross party lines." —Citizen Ronald Reagan's speech on behalf of Barry Goldwater's presidential candidacy in 1964.

I EXPECT THE first questions any reader would raise about *Why America Is Bankrupt* would be: "Who are you?" and "Why are you qualified to write this book?" Especially since much of this book concerns itself with what I call the "Black Subculture" or the BSC for short.

But before I list my many qualifications I must make a slight confession. I was going to call it the "Black Thug Culture" (BTC) instead of the "Black Subculture" (BSC) but then I started having second thoughts. Maybe "thug" was a bit too strong a word. Either way I am still going to be called a racist but why push it?

Then, just as I was having this debate with myself, I heard the black mayor of Baltimore call the people looting her city, "thugs." So I thought I was off the hook. But then she received a bunch of pushback for saying it. I was totally confused.

Then I heard a radio talk show host claim that blacks were now considering "thug" the new "N-word." So that sealed the deal. Even though I will list many examples of blacks themselves using the "thug" word, just as they use the "N-word," I will try to refrain from using it since I am living in the new America where "freedom of speech" has become merely a slogan.

Actually the BTC is really a sub-culture of the BSC. Many hard-working, law-abiding blacks living in BSC neighborhoods are just as upset about the BTC as white people are. So perhaps I will save the term Black Thug Culture (BTC) for only my most extreme examples. BSC or BTC, whatever, I hope I am not confusing you right out of the gate.

And please be forewarned that I will also touch on our illegal immigration problem since illegal immigrants are just like the BSC in many ways. For instance, both groups pay little in taxes yet each demands a myriad of free public services. They are both paving the road to our nation's bankruptcy in their own ways.

Now you may reasonably ask: "How do you have the nerve to proclaim yourself an expert on the plight of our black brothers and sisters?" Please let me explain.

I grew up in Cleveland, Ohio, in the 1950s when it was one of the largest and richest cities in a nation that was the richest, freest and most powerful country in the history of our planet. (Sorry if I repeat this mantra too many times.) In my youth I liked to brag that I lived in "the city" of Cleveland, as opposed to all the kids I met in college who grew up in "the suburbs." What I have witnessed in my home town over the past half century is the gristle from which this book was born.

The Cleveland of my youth was composed of a bunch of "poor skinny white kids" living on the west side and "poor skinny black kids" living on the east side. African Americans were only one of many ethnic groups in our city's melting pot. Sadly, thanks to the policies of the federal government over the years, Cleveland is now an ink pot populated primarily by African Americans.

I grew up in a unique neighborhood and was the product of a unique education. My neighborhood was a microcosm of the city. We had every nationality imaginable, even Native American Indians and Hispanics, but not blacks.

I went to a parochial grade school where we had 60 children in a classroom until 8th grade and everyone received a superior education, even the students with the poorest grades. Why? Because we did not have to deal with the BTC.

My street was only two streets away from one of the largest public housing projects in the city. I had to walk through what we called "the 'jects" four times a day because we came home for lunch. Not too many white kids would attempt that today. But I never had a problem. Why not? No BTC.

Then I went to an inner city public high school that was one of the largest high schools in our state AND the nation. Once again my high school was a microcosm of the city and we did have an African American segment that was just another ethnic group like all the other nationalities. Yet our attendance and graduation rates were both near 100 percent. And once again even the poorest students received a superior education that prepared them for a lifetime of valued employment. It also created the educated citizens who are essential for a participatory democracy. How did they do it? Easy, they did not have to deal with the BTC.

I will use examples from all of these experiences early and often in my essays to justify my views.

Upon graduating from high school I put myself through college working summers on the railroad as a "gandy dancer." I was the token white boy working on a track repair gang with a bunch of adult black men, mostly ex-cons. It was my first taste of the BSC and it was a great learning experience, not to mention a physical challenge.

For eight to ten hours a day we would swing sledge hammers (spike molls), tell stories and sing songs under the hot sun. I enjoyed working with them and I learned a lot from them. But I quickly understood that their neighborhoods were not like mine even though we all lived in the city of Cleveland. They needed guns, dogs and fences to protect their stuff from criminals while at work and even when watching TV in their own living rooms. Going out of town was a real risk for their property.

I, meanwhile, was living in Mayberry, USA. Because of my job I became friends with a very diverse (I love the word "diverse") cast of characters. One of my favorites was a guy who considered himself a real "ladies' man." Whenever we worked near one of the commuter train stations he would spy a young black mother with her baby. He would wander over by her and use his standard pick-up line.

"Hello, Mama, would you like a daddy for that baby?"

I was surprised by how effective it was. The next day he would usually regale us with stories of his latest conquest.

The first time I heard him do it I asked him if he was worried that the baby's real dad was going to be upset with him. He told me that the chances that the girl's baby had a dad at home were slim to none.

Looking back from today's perspective I now understand why the young ladies were so attracted to him. He had a J-O-B. I didn't think about this until much later but the last time we talked he still hadn't married any of them.

The ex-cons also told me another interesting fact that I did not think about until many years later. Most of them bragged that they had more than one Social Security number. It was easy to get a Social Security card back then. I just took my birth certificate down to the Federal office building in downtown Cleveland and they gave me one.

I'm sure they could make a fake birth certificate quite easily. I remember one college spring break in Fort Lauderdale where a kid was sitting in the back seat of his car pounding out fake draft cards on a portable typewriter so we tourists could pass for 21 years old, the drinking age in Florida. And they worked.

Why the other social security numbers? To collect more free benefits, of course. And many of them had personal injury lawsuits pending against the railroad. In other words, while they spent the day swinging heavy sledge hammers their lawyers were busy suing their employer claiming that they were eligible for disability benefits.

I was reminded of this when I read the *Plain Dealer* story by Associated Press reporter Stephen Ohlemacher on June 6, 2015, headlined: DISABILI-TY PROGRAM OVERPAID. It seems nearly half of the 9 million people receiving Social Security disability benefits over the last ten years were overpaid to the tune of $17 billion. And "the trust fund that supports the program is projected to run out of money late next year." I wonder if any of those guys also applied for Social Security disability?

I was amazed that they would even want to sue their employer. I was happy to just be receiving the steady paycheck. What a crazy system. When I asked them why they would want to sue the company that was putting food on their tables, they said they were just "getting over on the man, the railroad had deep pockets, it could afford it."

Those guys are probably all retired by now so I sometimes wonder how many of them are receiving retirement or disability benefits from more than one Social Security number. How many aliases do they have? (SSDAS) No wonder our Social Security system is almost broke.

Anyway, this is how I began to understand what the BSC is all about. In many ways my "gandy dancer" railroad experience was more educational than my college courses.

After college I travelled the world and eventually came back home. I then worked a string of widely "diverse" jobs to support my fledging freelance writing career. My jobs contributed as much to my education as my high school teachers and college professors.

But it was my job as a substitute teacher in the "City of Cleveland" (not the suburbs) public school system that brought me back full circle to the BSC. I returned to my old high school during the height of the school busing experiment and experienced firsthand how the BSC destroyed what was once one of the best public schools systems in the country.

On top of that I have actually lived in neighborhoods that flipped from white middle class to black subculture dominance. It is not a pretty sight. But I learned a lot about the BSC in the process.

Eventually I became a "City of Cleveland" (not the suburbs) fire fighter. And I spent my first 20 years as a fireman working in BSC neighborhoods. There again I learned about the BSC up close and personal. There were also many racial issues within the department that opened my eyes considerably.

But the real reason that I am uniquely qualified to write this book is that I have been paying taxes since I first entered the work force as a 16-year-old in 1965. That was the same year that President Lyndon B. Johnson invented "The Great Society."

Johnson was already busy expanding the Vietnam War. He could not really afford to do that. But it did not stop him from creating all these new government programs like Medicare and Medicaid and The Department of Housing and Urban Development (HUD). The idea was to eliminate poverty in our lifetime. Sorry, but it didn't work. In fact, it did just the opposite. It increased poverty exponentially while at the same time creating what I call the Black Subculture (BSC).

(See my chapter about "The War on Poverty.")

The BSC is composed of all the people, mostly African Americans, who have been living in my home town the same time I have but who have never worked or paid any taxes over the last 50 years. And U.S. government has been taking my tax payments and giving it to them for all these years.

(I will explain this more thoroughly in my "Where Our Taxes Go" chapter.)

This is why America is bankrupt. We should all be mad as hell that our great nation is up to its armpits in debt because it has to support a culture that is totally dependent on the government for its survival. That is Communism people.

To make a long story short, in my lifetime I have witnessed the decline and decay of my once great neighborhood, my once great city, my once great public school system and I now fear, my once great nation.

And what is the common thread, the ultimate cause of all this dysfunction? Very simply: "The Black Subculture." We need to dismantle it. And who is responsible for creating the BSC? The federal government, specifically the Democrat Party, that's who.

Fortunately, most white Americans live in areas where they are not yet affected by the BSC. Most have never even driven through a BSC neighborhood. They have never experienced the boarded-up buildings and drug dealers hanging outside the corner store.

Unfortunately, those days are quickly coming to an end. The BSC is coming to a neighborhood near you so you best be prepared.

That is why I wrote this book. To give America a strong and loud wake-up call. And I feel that I am qualified to write it because besides being an author and an historian, I have also experienced our nation's fiscal failings up close and personal.

I hope you learn as much reading it as I did writing it.

CHAPTER THREE:
WHY AMERICA IS BANKRUPT

"First, we'll have your tax cut, then we'll have my expenditures program,"—President John F. Kennedy to his economic advisor Walter Heller in 1962.

I UNDERSTAND THAT reading about debt problems is about as exciting as reading your monthly credit card statement. The urge is to throw it in the wastepaper basket and hope they forget to send next month's bill. Believe me, writing about debt and bankruptcy is about as sexy as watching paint dry. But someone has to do it before our children drown in it.

So let me take you back to the 1960s when all our massive debt problems began. It was about the same time that I entered the work force. The economy was sluggish when our bright, young, energetic Democratic President John F. Kennedy was elected in 1960. He wanted to do something about it so he brought together a team of highly educated economic advisors to figure out what to do. These academics were part of what would later be called "the best and the brightest." I'll talk more about them later but for now let's look at some of their ideas.

Like I said the introduction, I don't want to bore you with economic theories and graphs and charts and numbers. I want to show you how these economic policies played out on the mean streets of Cleveland, Ohio. So let me summarize their views in layman's terms.

Kennedy's advisors debated two different ways to jump start our nation's economy. One way was to cut taxes. This would put more money in the hands of our citizens who would buy more things which in turn would create more jobs as more people would be needed to create more things to buy. Catch my drift?

The downside of a tax cut is that there would be less money to run the government, less money for things like paying government employees, buying military airplanes and building rocket ships.

The second theory was the direct government funding of programs that would be used to hire more workers. These workers would also then have the money to buy more things and create more jobs building more things to buy. This is what President Franklin Delano Roosevelt did to help get us out of the Great Depression. He created all the "alphabet programs" like the Civilian Conservation Corps (CCC) and the Tennessee Valley Authority (TVA). Kennedy ramped up the National Aeronautics and Space Administration (NASA). But once again the government would need money it did not have to fund these new programs.

Either way the problem was how to pay for the economic stimulus? So Kennedy's advisors, led by Walter Heller, followed the advice of a previous economist, John Maynard Keynes, the father of "Keynesian economics."

Heller proposed something called "deficit funding." He proposed borrowing ten billion dollars to keep the government working during the transition. It was a huge amount of money at the time but merely pocket change to today's politicians.

The idea was that the government would borrow the money for now but once the economy started rolling again the tax income would increase and the government could pay off its debt.

Sounds good on paper, right? So did the Vietnam War. The problem is that once the politicians in Washington have money to spend they never worry about paying it back. Let the next congress or president concern themselves with those silly details.

So Kennedy ended up doing both tax cuts and government programs.

Here's how David Greenberg of *Slate.com* explained it in a 2004 article titled "Tax Cuts in Camelot":

"Kennedy, it turns out, initially wanted to use government spending, not tax cuts, as the means to put dollars in people's hands. But that idea ran aground in 1962 because conservatives in Congress opposed it....Still, even as Kennedy accepted tax reduction as the first step along the route to growth, he never gave up his spending idea. 'First, we'll have your tax cut,' he told Heller; 'then we'll have my expenditures program.'"

So that's how our national debt rose from $310 billion under President Kennedy to $18 trillion under President Obama.

Of course Kennedy had a lot of help from his successors. Each succeeding President did his part to increase our debt. But it was LBJ who used this "deficit spending" idea to fund both the Vietnam War and his "War on Poverty." And we lost them both.

It is Kennedy's "deficit spending" mindset that still permeates Washington today. Before him, we tried to live within our means except in times of war.

"To contract new debts is not the way to pay old ones."—George Washington, our nation's first and greatest president, The Father of Our Country, in a letter to James Welch, April 7, 1799.

I used this quote to open my book. We should have heeded George Washington's advice about not taking out new debts to pay off old ones. It is the dirty little secret in Washington D.C. that two hundred years later America is bankrupt. We are trillions of dollars in debt and our debt is growing by billions of dollars every day. Yet I personally heard President

Barak Obama take credit for actually lowering "the deficit," whatever that means. This is Washington gobbledygook at its finest.

Just paying the interest on our loans consumes huge amounts of our nation's wealth. What a tragedy this is for our children and grandchildren. Besides, they are up to their elbows in debt themselves. Josh Lederman of the Associated Press wrote on March 11, 2015: "The government estimates total U.S. student debt exceeds $1.1 trillion, with about 7 million Americans in default." It looks like our children learned from their politicians about paying down their debts. They will be paying off these loans for decades to come.

Here's another great example of the mess we find ourselves in.

The magazine *The Week* reported in its February 20, 2015 issue that "by 2021, the White House forecasts, the U.S. will be spending more on interest for the national debt than on the entire defense budget. (*WSJ.com*)" This is straight from the White House. Is anyone listening out there?

Now add this to the mix. Kevin G. Hall of the *Tribune* Washington Bureau reported on March 9, 2015 that: "After years of debt that normally amounted to about a third of the nation's total economy, it has spiked to more than 70 percent with no relief in sight."

He adds: "The nonpartisan Congressional Budget Office...sees the debt level approaching 80 percent in 2025...Just eight years ago this number was about 35 percent, about the historical average."

Thank you, President Barack Obama. Hall says: "Debt went from $7.5 trillion in 2009 to $12.6 trillion in 2014 under Obama." Now it is closer to $18 trillion. And he still has two more years in office.

And here is an even scarier number. We only take in about $1.4 trillion a year in taxes. Yet the last time I looked we owe China and Japan over $1.2 trillion each. How are we ever supposed to pay them off?

Does anyone in D.C. understand what a HUGE, HUGE number a trillion is? What the hell is going on in Washington? What happens when our debt equals 100 percent of our income and all our wealth goes to paying our debtors? There will be nothing left to run the country. That day is approaching at breakneck speed. Our economic engine is a freight train running on the tracks to a national disaster.

The sad thing is that Hall quotes government economists who say that our debt at 75 percent of our Gross Domestic Product is "the new normal." And they blame the baby boomers for this dire forecast. Why? Because there are so many of us who now want all the money back that we paid into the system.

Well, I don't know about you, my friendly reader, but I am a proud baby boomer. I started working at 16 years old and worked my entire adult life, often at two or more jobs. So did most of my friends and family.

What have our fearless leaders been doing with all the money we gave them? I'll tell you what, throwing it away on useless social programs that are counterproductive to their aims. If our federal government were a private industry it would have declared bankruptcy a long time ago, fired all of its employees and started all over again from scratch.

Our representatives in Washington are out of control. Americans should be mad as hell at what our professional politicians have been doing with our tax dollars for the last half century. But most of us don't have a clue as to how they are giving away the riches in our treasury.

The object of this book is to shake our citizens out of their complacency so they will act to save our once great nation.

Our professional politicians do not want the American public to understand our crippling debt and how it impacts our nation. So they just keep printing more money and raising our nation's debt limit every time it is due. That is what they do in the banana republics of South America. Eventually your money becomes worthless. In some countries their paper currency became so worthless that they actually used it for toilet paper. Is that what we want for the American dollar?

Our politicians have been acting like drunken spendthrifts. It is like they have been applying for a new two billion dollar credit card every day before they start work in the morning. You try doing that and see how long it flies.

They are afraid that if someone notices the dire straits that we are in, they will all lose their cozy jobs. They have no plan on how to pay off our debt or any idea of how we got here. So they keep kicking the problem down the road hoping the next administration will figure something out.

Our current president, Barack Hussein Obama, is an expert at playing this game. He has added trillions of dollars to our national debt yet he never saw a government spending program he did not embrace.

He lashes out at "income inequality" and he condemns "the evil one percent" of our citizens who sit on the top of our economic system even though he is a charter member. Like the rest of the Democratic Party he pretends to be a champion of the poor while filling his pockets with the taxpayer's money. And don't even get me going on Hillary Clinton.

The purpose of my book is really a quite simple one. I will show you, my curious readers, how the Democratic Party over the last half century sold its soul in order to attract, create and keep black voters in its fold. And how in doing so it transformed our great cities from economic job creating engines into welfare collecting federally subsidized sinkholes and in the process bankrupted and weakened the once wealthy and powerful United States of America.

This book is part memoir, part history textbook and part economic thesis. Sadly many of our citizens are not much interested in history and economics, finding them too boring. So I will attempt to explain in simple and hopefully entertaining terms why it is very important that you understand what has changed in our country since the mid-twentieth century. Voters, especially young voters, both black and white, need to understand how the policies championed by the Democratic Party have crippled our nation, its security and its future.

Hard-working white voters need to understand how the Democrats used our taxes to attract black voters by promising them loads of free stuff. Black voters need to understand what will happen when the well runs dry and the government runs out of free stuff because the Democrats gave it all away. The Democrats spent billions of dollars creating what I call the Black Subculture (BSC) which in turn sucks billions of dollars out of our economy.

And where is the BSC primarily located? In our nation's inner cities. And who has been in control of all of our nation's big cities since the 1960s? The Democratic Party, that's who. Almost all the politicians in our major cities for the past 50 years have been Democrats. And what have they accomplished besides lining their pockets with taxpayers money? Absolutely nothing. As our city's black neighborhoods riot again, just like in the 1960s, it is easy to see that nothing has changed.

Maybe my black brothers and sisters should try something different, like voting for a Republican now and then, to keep the politicians honest.

My book is different than your standard history textbook in a number of ways. First of all, I will not only show what happened to our once great nation but I will provide actual solutions to our most pressing problems. We need to act swiftly before we become just another third world country that cannot feed its citizens or protect itself from its enemies.

I am hoping this book will light a fire under my fellow baby boomers. Seventy-five million of us were born here from 1946-1964. We were blessed to grow up in such a wonderful environment, the freest, richest, most powerful country in the history of our planet.

So we went to work and paid our taxes and funded programs like Social Security, Medicare and Medicaid for over 50 years. Our country should be awash in cash instead of straddled by staggering debt.

Now there are 10,000 of us retiring every day. I throw this challenge to all of us. We have the numbers, we have the time and we can still make a difference. Let us work together to make sure our children and grand-children can experience the same great United States of America that we grew up in.

CHAPTER FOUR:
THE SOLUTION

"Ohio members of Congress spent their campaign money on everything from tickets to movies, the Cleveland Cavaliers and Indians games to fundraising trips to California, Las Vegas and Miami Beach."—Sabrina Eaton in a Cleveland Plain Dealer *story on April 20, 2015, headlined* CONGRESS CAMPAIGN CASH GOES FOR ALL SORTS OF STUFF

THE SOLUTION TO all our economic problems is really quite simple. The government needs to take in more money and spend less money until we balance our books. The hard part is having our president and Congress figure out how to do it when so much of our income goes to servicing our huge debt. The only solution our current leaders offer is to keep raising our debt limit and passing on our problems to the next generation.

So in this chapter I am going to provide the reader with an array of solutions to change our government's structure so it can grapple with the grave problems facing our nation. Then I will spend the rest of the book explaining why we need these solutions. I realize that it is a somewhat backward approach but I wanted to put the solutions up front because I know how short the attention spans are for many readers, especially our younger ones.

The easiest way to put us on the path to solvency is also quite simple. It is time for our government to stop subsidizing what I term the Black Subculture (BSC). The cost is huge and the consequences are frightening.

Once this is done our treasury would once again start taking in more money than it is spending, a great accomplishment.

But it will be very difficult to transform the Black Subculture (BSC) into the Black Prosperous Culture (BPC) without making fundamental changes to the way Washington works. You would think most blacks would be in favor of eliminating the ghetto neighborhoods that exist in most of our big cities.

But to do that we need to stop creating the criminals who are responsible for most of our big city crime, the dysfunction of our big city schools and the huge cost of our big city justice systems. This would make black neighborhoods much more livable and their homes more valuable. I believe that once my black brothers and sisters understand my views they will agree with them.

It would also help to eliminate racism in our country, both black and white. Racism was disappearing within my generation, the baby boomers, when I was growing up. Then the federal government anointed African Americans as "the government approved minority," thus creating the BSC. It is very difficult for anyone who must deal with the BSC on a daily basis, like the cops on inner city streets, to not become racist. And it goes both ways.

Of course I am not proposing that we just stop giving benefits to the great many of our citizens who already receive them. I am NOT suggesting we just throw them out into the streets. Not only would that be heartless, it would lead to economic chaos.

Of course, we need a safety net for our citizens to make it through tough times. But the "safety net" has become a cradle to grave lifestyle in our BSC. What we need is to let the BSC wither on its vine. It will take a couple generations to succeed but at least we will be on the trail to prosperity. And to do that we will need the help of both our black and white American citizens. Here's why.

The BSC is draining our treasury of its wealth at a staggering rate. I will show the details of this phenomenon in another chapter. But let it be said right here and now that we desperately need to quit producing United States citizens who never pay a penny in taxes from their cradle to their grave yet suck up thousands of dollars a year in social benefits and related expenses. Once you realize that we have created millions of these poor citizens then you can imagine their huge drain on our government's resources.

I will also explain in future chapters how the Democrats created and exploited the Black Subculture for their benefit. And how in doing so they crippled our great country. But before I do so I want to first show how hard it will be to change the direction of our nation and what must be done to accomplish this mighty task.

We will need to make fundamental changes to our system of government before it will be able to make fundamental changes to our welfare system. The reason we are at this important crossroad is that our Congress has become a group of professional politicians. They are a bunch of men and women who are more concerned about keeping their sweet spots than they are about the welfare of our nation. They are too entrenched in our present political system to tackle the huge task before us. We are in desperate need of new blood and new ideas.

So before we can enact the changes I am proposing we must first replace the professional politicians who created this mess in the first place. This will not be an easy task. Public service should be a sacrifice like it was for our Founding Fathers, not the cash cow that it has become today.

We need to change the culture of Washington D.C. Sadly, we can no longer do that through elections. The culture is too ingrained, so we need to change its structure.

So I am proposing three major changes to our political system. They are such fundamental changes that the only way to accomplish them is to add three new amendments to our great U.S. Constitution. Thankfully our Founding Fathers gave us this option long, long ago.

But before I list my proposals let me talk about another amendment that is being discussed today, the balanced budget amendment. While it has worked for state governments like in my home state, Ohio, it is not practical for the federal government.

Why not? Because our federal government is charged with the responsibility of protecting our borders and as such must sometimes declare war on our enemies. Depending on the circumstances, we may need to borrow money quickly and not be hampered by a balanced budget amendment. Besides, the bookkeepers in D.C. are too good at making the numbers sound much better than they really are. They could tell us our budget is balanced and not even be close.

So back to my amendments. We must also understand that it is not easy to change our Constitution which is actually a good thing. All our amendments to date have been ratified by state legislatures after being proposed by Congress.

We need two thirds of both houses of Congress to propose an amendment. But when it comes to changing their own power structure, that is not going to happen. The inmates aren't going to reform the asylum.

The other alternative is for the states to call a "constitutional convention." Then we need two thirds of our state legislatures to propose the amendment which must be ratified by three-fourths of state legislatures.

This is also very difficult. We would need a lot of agreement that the changes are in the best interests of our nation.

An easier method would be to just make sure before we elect anyone to Congress they promise to make these reforms. And if they don't keep their promise we don't re-elect them and elect someone who will.

Now that I have you totally confused let us look at the amendments to the U.S. Constitution that I am proposing.

First, we need term limits for our U.S. representatives, senators and president. Second, we need to redesign the United States of America. By that I mean to change the geography of our states so that they truly reflect our citizen's votes. As part of that amendment I also propose that we move our nation's capital from Washington D.C. to somewhere in the middle of the country like Kansas or Iowa.

We will also need a third amendment changing the definition of an American citizen. This is needed to address our illegal immigration crisis.

After we make these major changes in our political system, then we can work on some of the other solutions I will propose, like an overhaul of our tax system, a truly secured southern border and a minimum wage hike that matters. By that I mean one for professions like teachers and doctors instead of fast food workers.

How are we going to accomplish all these radical ideas? Please hear me out.

First, let's discuss term limits. They work in many states like in my Ohio and they would work well for the federal government. The solutions to the long range effects of the BSC are simple ones. But Congress will never take any action as it is presently organized. The Democratic Party relies too heavily on its black voters for its existence to dare make any changes that will upset the BSC. And since half our country's white voters go Democrat and half go Republican, the Republicans will never have enough votes to overhaul the system by themselves. Besides, there are too many professional politicians on both sides of the aisle who would never want to upset the apple cart.

I read recently that, for the first time, more than half the members of Congress are millionaires. There is nothing wrong with that if they were millionaires before they came to Congress and put their careers on hold to dedicate themselves to public service. That's what our founding fathers did. In fact, they took a great risk on possibly losing their lives and fortunes to create our blessed democracy. Instead too many of today's congressmen and women are professional politicians who have enriched themselves at the public trough for decades and the last thing they want to do is abdicate their powerful positions. We have become way too similar to third world countries. This is not the United States of America of my youth.

My proposal is a very simple one. We need term limits so the professional politicians cannot spend their lifetimes padding their pockets. Here are a couple of examples from many to prove my point. One from each side of the aisle.

Democratic senator Ted Kennedy died in office after spending 47 years in the Senate. Republican senator Strom Thurman served for 48 years after switching parties in 1964. He was still a senator at age 100. Both were shadows of their former selves at the end of their careers but our voters kept electing them because incumbents have a huge advantage the way our election system is presently arranged. Once they are entrenched in office they never leave unless they are caught in some extreme scandal. Shame on us for continually voting these losers back into office.

Here is what I propose. We need a constitutional amendment that limits each branch of Congress to only six years of service. Then you are term limited out. Many states like my native Ohio already have similar rules and it works just fine for them. At the very least you will have to elect a new batch of criminals every so often. Spread the wealth so to speak.

This means only three two-year terms in the House of Representatives. After your six-year gig you're out. If you want to continue serving in Congress it would behoove you to do a good job in the House so that the voters will let you continue your political career as a senator. But you are limited to only one six year term in the Senate. That's twelve years on the public trough. After that you will have to find a real job.

Now for the president. The president will only be allowed to serve one four-year term for the same reasons. Today our fearless leader spends much of his first four years in office campaigning for his second term. This would eliminate all that wasted effort.

It would also make his choice of vice president much more meaning-ful. The presidential candidate would want to have a running mate who shares his or her beliefs and would be ready to run for the office himself in four years instead of just choosing a vice president for geographic balance on the ticket.

Benjamin Franklin, our nation's elder statesman and the brains behind our innovative democratic system, wanted term limits at the beginning of our great nation. He thought it was a good idea for our politicians to return to civilian life and have to live under the laws they passed. They had just won their independence from a tyrannical monarchy and he didn't want it replaced with another one. It was only George Washington's enormous popularity that persuaded him otherwise. Fortunately, Washington had enough sense to step down after his second term even though he probably could have kept the job for life. His example of two four-year terms became the norm until our nation asked Democrat Franklin D. Roosevelt to keep the job for four terms because we didn't want to change horses in the middle of World War II.

However, Roosevelt's long reign scared Republicans enough to ratify the Twenty-second Amendment in 1951 that limited future presidents to two terms in office.

We need to cut that back to one term. Our country has over 320 million citizens. I'm sure we can find another great leader to replace even the best of them. And if we do elect a loser like Obama by mistake it is much easier to replace him.

While we are at it we also need to add some language to this amend-ment prohibiting our president's relatives from running for office. I liked President George W. Bush but I didn't like the fact that he was the son of President George H. W. Bush. Now we are faced with the possibility of former President Bill Clinton's wife, Hillary Clinton, running against President Bush's brother, Jeb Bush, in 2016.

This is what they do in third world dictatorships. They pass the leadership role to wives and children to keep their power and stolen wealth in the family. It is no different than the European monarchies of the past. We are in the twenty-first century and there is no reason that in a country of 320 million citizens we cannot find fresh new leaders every four years.

For example, look at the 2016 Republican candidates for president. We have over a dozen excellent potential presidents. It should be like that every four years.

If we amend the Constitution and enact these rules it will help safeguard our Congress from becoming a den of thieves. Of course we would have to elect only one third of the seats at time so that there is not a whole new government every four years. You need some kind of continuity.

Maybe we can even find a group of true "public servants" who sacrifice their careers and families to lead us like our Founding Fathers did, instead of the professional politicians who are enriching themselves on our labor today.

Now here is my second proposed new amendment to our great Constitution. We need to redesign the map of the United States of America. Why? Because the original 13 states have way too much power in the halls of Congress.

Have you ever taken a hard look at the map of our great country? A state like Rhode Island, that is about the same size as Cuyahoga County where I live, has two senators, the same as the huge states of Texas and California. So do many of the other little states on the east coast like Connecticut and Delaware. No wonder our laws have an east coast left wing liberal bias.

You need to understand just how powerful the United States Senate is. In many ways it has as much power in shaping our country's fortunes as the president. Who we send to represent us shapes our nation for years to come.

Yet Rhode Island, with a population of about a million, has two senators just like California, with a population of 38 million. The last time I checked, one out of every eight Americans lived in California. Something is wrong here that needs to be updated.

So here is what I propose. I live in Ohio, which has a bit over ten million residents. That's just about the right size for a state. Ohio has cities and farms and rivers and lakes and hills and valleys. That's why it is considered one of the most important states in presidential elections. On Election Day we are a good predicator of the rest of the country. The way Ohio votes tells us a lot about the eventual outcome of our presidential election.

What I propose is that we create a nation of states all about the size of Ohio. We take New Hampshire, Vermont, Massachusetts, Connecticut and Rhode Island and make one state out of them. Then we take Maryland, Delaware, and New Jersey and throw in the District of Columbia and make one state of out them.

Including D.C. will give all those east coast liberals a good taste of the BSC that they admire from afar as long as they don't have to deal with it up close and personal. This will also solve the District of Columbia's long time argument that it does not have any true representation in Congress.

Now we have changed eight of our original 13 states into two. We would have to make up six states to get back to 50. Or we could only add four new ones to return to the 48 states that we had when I was a kid, before we added Alaska and Hawaii.

Next you have to look at the state's populations. Our four most populated states are California, Florida, Texas and New York. California has almost four times the citizens as the second tier of states like Ohio,

Illinois and Pennsylvania. Florida, Texas and New York have about twice as many.

So I propose that we split California into Northern and Southern California much like North and South Carolina or North and South Dakota. California's population is so huge it deserves four senators, not two. And since California is one of our most liberal states the liberal East Coast states that it is replacing should be easily appeased.

Florida's population is also huge so we should create a Northern Florida and a Southern Florida. Now they also have four senators instead of two.

Texas is another huge state in both land mass and population. So I propose we split Texas in half, creating an East Texas and a West Texas, kind of like West Virginia and Virginia.

Next is New York. New York City is the great population mix in that state. So we need an East New York and a West New York state. Once again four senators instead of two.

So now we have four new states to replace the six we eliminated. We are back to 48 states which is the number I learned when I was growing up. I believe the new configuration of the United States of America would be much more representative of our citizens' wishes than the one we have now.

Of course the small East Coast states will fight this idea tooth and nail. No one wants to give up their power without a fight. It will be up to the rest of us to convince them that they must for the public good. This is the beauty of the Constitution being amended by the vote of three quarters of the states. Sometimes the majority must impose its will on the minority. This is our democratic system, the majority rules.

Besides, there is a precedent in our history for such actions. Look at the splitting up of the Northwest Territory, or West Virginia splitting from Virginia, or Vermont splitting from New York. There is even a movement afoot by some western New York state counties to secede from

New York and join Pennsylvania because of fracking. Let's give it a go and see how it flies.

As part of that amendment there is another major change that I am proposing for our great country. It may not need to be part of the Constitutional amendment, maybe just an amendment to the Residence Act of 1790 which created our nation's capital. I'll let the Constitutional lawyers figure that one out.

I propose moving our nation's capital from Washington D.C. to somewhere in the middle of our country like Kansas or Iowa. Why? Because when our Founding Fathers first picked the D.C. area it WAS the middle of our country. But of course it is no longer.

There is a lot of open space in the cornfields of the Midwest where we could drop a bunch of new government buildings. I believe this is necessary for a number of reasons.

First there is the obvious one. We need to eliminate the beltway culture that stretches from New York City, our media capital, to Washington, our political capital. Those members of the media and the Congress who spend all their time on the beltway are completely out of touch with the rest of our citizens.

New York City and Washington D.C. have about as much to do with the rest of our great nation as Baghdad or Tehran. We need our capital to be relocated to an area where our representatives will be immersed in a culture of Midwestern common sense.

Call me prejudiced because I'm from Ohio but we don't buy a lot of the nonsense that comes out of Washington as gospel. But they like to shove it down our throats and tell us that we are too ignorant to know what's good for us. Too many times in my lifetime I've witnessed "do gooders" in Washington force their ideas on Ohio and it's always ended with huge unintended consequences and always for the worse. Can you say the Vietnam War, forced school busing, affirmative action or Obamacare?

These were all products of Democratic administrations. If our leaders were surrounded by a bit more Midwestern pragmatism maybe a little of it would rub off on them.

Then there is the problem of national security. Our enemies in Europe and the Middle East grow bolder every day. Moving our capital to the middle of the country would make it much easier to defend it if our country was ever attacked from the east or the west. It may seem far-fetched today but who knows what the world will look like 20, 50, even a hundred years from now.

It is better to plan now than be caught with our pants down as we were on December 7, 1941, and September 11, 2001. Our capital would be cushioned by a huge land mass as well as two great oceans. Not many countries have such a luxury. We should take advantage of it while we can.

What would we do with all our great buildings in Washington D.C.? Easy. Turn them into museums honoring our great country. Many of them already are monuments, such as the Washington, Lincoln and Jefferson monuments. We need to downsize our federal government anyway. Build a few nice buildings on some open land in Kansas and let the government work out of them. Give the president Harry Truman's old house or build him a nice new White House with all the latest electronic stuff. Without the opulent residence maybe future presidents would become more practical and less regal.

These are the three major changes I am proposing for our Constitution. Once we have changed the complexion of our Congress then we can begin to act on some of my other ideas, like tax reform, reverse immigration and real minimum wage hikes.

For example, we are also going to need another Constitutional amendment that addresses our immigration problem.

Very simply, we need to change the definition of an American citizen from simply someone who is born in the United States of America. We need a rider to that idea which states that anyone born in the USA must also have two parents who are either American citizens or LEGAL immigrants.

This will dry up all the pregnant illegals that sneak across the border just in time to drop their babies here so they can receive free medical care and their families can qualify for loads of free stuff just like the BSC. (Immigration reform will have its own chapter later.)

We also need to redesign the makeup of our great cities. Way back in 1996 I wrote an op-ed piece for the Cleveland *Plain Dealer* on the 200th anniversary of the founding of the city of Cleveland. I suggested the city had outgrown its function and that it was time to break up the corrupt, racially divided structure into six suburbs.

Thankfully, the suburbs still provided its citizens with valuable services while the city of Cleveland did not. An important offshoot of my plan would have been the breaking up of the Cleveland school system, a dismal failure at educating our children since the forced school busing disaster.

But no one took me up on my idea and twenty years later we still have a Cleveland public school system that does not educate our children. (More on this subject in the school busing chapter.)

We could have been the model for solving all our nation's inner city ills. For example, New York City could have turned its five boroughs into five small cities. Smaller government is better. The suburbs work, our big cities do not. Look at the riots in them today. This was a very simple solution to a very complex set of problems.

Am I presenting you with too much to handle all at once, my patient reader? Does this all sound a bit too crazy? Please read on, my trusted citizens, for I will explain what pushed our once great nation to the verge of bankruptcy and what we can do about it. Here are my views in more detail.

CHAPTER FIVE:
THERE GOES THE NEIGHBORHOOD

"What is important here, however, is to cultivate a greater focus on the damn punks who terrorize American streets. While it is currently en vogue *to demonize police, America's inner cities teem with ruthless young men who routinely kill and maim with a shocking disregard for life—and not because of some twisted political motive." -Phillip Morris, an African American columnist for the Cleveland* Plain Dealer.

AMERICA IS A country of neighborhoods. We have two types of neighborhoods in America today. The one kind goes to work every day, pays it taxes, supports our democracy and keeps its property values up. The second kind stays home, lives off government handouts, pays few taxes and watches its property values plummet.

The question I want everyone who reads my book to ask is: "What kind of neighborhood do you want to live in?" I hope that reading this book will help you answer that question.

This book is about what has happened to the neighborhoods in our big cities over the past half century. We are on the road to destruction and no one seems to care

In the next few chapters I am going to explain to you in great detail what the Black Subculture (BSC) is all about and how it is bankrupting America. When I am finished I hope you will understand that the BSC is more of a threat to our nation's security than the Islamic State of Iraq and

Syria (ISIS). The reason that none of our leaders are addressing this problem is out of fear of being labeled "racist."

I do not have that fear so I am going to explain to you how the many different government programs that support the BSC cost us billions of dollars, directly and indirectly. Our present system is placing our democracy in jeopardy for future generations.

As I mentioned earlier, I also hope that I do not offend many of you by calling the black troublemakers who populate the Black Thug Culture (BTC) within the BSC, "thugs." You may have missed it because the media kind of let it slip away but our esteemed African American United States Attorney General, Eric Holder, called them "punks."

He used the term to describe the black youth who shot and injured two white police officers in Ferguson, Missouri during the protests. (Since this action did not receive anywhere near as much publicity as the white cop who shot the black kid you may have missed this.) A twenty-year-old black youth, Jeffrey Williams, was arrested for the crime.

The *New York Times* described him as an unemployed male who lives with his pregnant girlfriend and spends his time playing and betting on video basketball games.

Eric Holder described him as a "damn punk." So did Phillip Morris, the African American columnist for the *Plain Dealer*. That was a word that we baby boomers tossed around in our youth. I am going with "thug" because it is a bit more current.

So here we go. Here is my thesis on "The Black Subculture" (BSC).

The first and most dangerous pillar of the BSC is Section 8 housing because it is the great neighborhood destroyer. I'll explain Section 8 in much detail later but for now let me just warn you of this. If you look out your window and see a sign that says: "FOR RENT, Section 8 Okay," on your neighbor's lawn, you can kiss your neighborhood good-bye.

That is the reason for the old saying: "There Goes The Neighborhood." I will get down and dirty with details later. But first let me tell you a story. It is about my first contact with the Black Subculture.

It was the early 1980s and I was newly married. My grandmother had passed away and I bought the family homestead off her estate. It wasn't much of a homestead but I wasn't making that much money. The neighborhood was filled with what are called "two family duplexes," or starter houses.

We lived on the first floor and rented an identical second floor to another family. Both families shared the attic and basement. This type of housing was typical for the city of Cleveland but you don't see many such structures in the suburbs.

My grandma's house was located in Cleveland's inner city. It was the house my grandparents lived in when they raised six children during the depths of the Great Depression. After moving in I often thought about my dad's childhood. How could eight people live in such cramped quarters? There were only two bedrooms and they didn't even have doors, just a couple of wooden rods with curtains.

Even crazier was that another full family with who knows how many kids was living in the second half of the house above them. How crowded was that family? And then there were the other kids in the neighborhood who just liked to hang around the Jedick household. When my grandmother died quite a few of them introduced themselves to me at her funeral and told me they spent most of their time at my grandma's house because their own homes were a bit dysfunctional.

All in all, it must have been quite a madhouse. Especially when eight of them were fighting for the one bathroom. I was told my grandfather killed live chickens in the basement and the kids would have to pluck the feathers. My grandmother would make homemade bread, her own noodles and chicken soup. It fed the family for a week. They also had a peach tree in the backyard that my grandmother canned the peaches from. It provided them with fruit all winter long.

My grandfather's family were school teachers in the old country, Eastern Europe. It was a highly respected position in their village. Yet my grandfather came to America and started off working in a coal mine just to taste the air of freedom. Back then working in a coal mine was pure hell. You could not stand up straight all day, chipping away at hard rocks with a pick and never seeing the sun from its rise to its setting.

Coming to Cleveland and working on the railroad was heaven compared to that. His family never received food stamps, utility relief or rent subsidies but they did just fine. All six of their children went on to lead successful lives. They raised families of their own, paid their share of taxes, served in the military, bought homes and contributed to our nation's overall wellbeing.

So I was following in their footsteps. At about the time we moved in the local media was calling young couples like us "urban pioneers." They said there was a movement going on where young couples were buying inner city houses and invigorating the old neighborhoods. If that trend was allowed to continue without the federal government's interference, without school busing, without Section 8 housing, without a "government approved" minority, the City of Cleveland would still be a wonderful place to live.

Today they call homes like ours "low income housing." The house was already over 70 years old but the price was right for a couple newlyweds and I knew the neighborhood. It was mostly populated by older people like my grandmother who lived there all their lives and owned their homes. But the neighborhood was changing.

The rent from the upstairs tenants helped me pay the mortgage. That's how my grandparents made it through the Depression. My grandmother had trouble maintaining the family landmark as she aged so the house was in need of major repairs. I ended up remodeling the entire inside. I didn't have much money but I had friends in the building trades and I helped them with the grunt work. It is called investing "sweat equity" in your property. By the time I was finished I probably had the nicest interior in the neighborhood.

I liked the neighborhood. The old ethnic ladies who knew my grand-mother liked to spoil my two young children. We lived near the Cleveland Zoo and I could walk there with my children at any time. Next to the Zoo was Brookside Park, a large open area with a neighborhood pool, where my kids could romp. All was good in the neighborhood.

Then one day I was raking leaves in my front yard and I noticed an old lady who reminded me of my grandmother walking down our street. She came from the corner bus stop towing a wire food basket behind her. If you have never seen one, it is a tall metal basket on two wheels that carries food from the market. That was how my grandmother fed her six children. She never owned a car. She took two buses to the West Side Market and dragged the food home. It was not an easy life.

As the old lady was walking suddenly two young black kids came out of nowhere and started harassing her. They were trying to steal the food out of her basket and she was struggling with them. This was the first time I ever saw black people in our neighborhood. Cleveland was a pretty segregated city at the time. Most of the black neighborhoods were on the east side of the Cuyahoga River which cuts Cleveland in half. The west side was mostly white families.

So I dropped my rake and went over to help the old white lady. I told the black kids to leave her alone. They ran away, into a house across the street. I later learned they were renting the upstairs half. (Thank you, Section 8 housing subsidy.) The old lady thanked me and went on her way. I went back to raking my leaves and wondered when the black kids had moved into the neighborhood. It was one of the few houses where I did not know the owner. Someone must have bought it as an investment property. Absentee landlords are the scourge of any neighborhood. (In 2008 they would cause what President Obama likes to call "The Great Recession" but that is another story.)

A few minutes later a Cleveland police car pulled into my driveway. The police officer wanted to talk to me. I thought maybe the old lady called the cops on the kids. Wrong. The kid's mother, who I would never see as long as I lived in the neighborhood, called the cops on me. The policeman told me that she filed a complaint that I was harassing her children.

So I told the policeman what really happened. I also told him that I couldn't believe the kid's mom called the cops on me. When I was growing up if my parents heard that I gave an old person a hard time I would have been punished severely. Fortunately, the police officer agreed with me. But he explained to me that the times have changed. This was my first experience with a black person playing the race card, long before O.J. Simpson used it to get out of jail free.

Then he gave me a piece of advice that I remember to this day.

"If it's your word against hers you're going to lose," he told me.

I couldn't believe it.

"So what am I supposed to do?" I asked him.

"Move," he said.

And he was right. That's what white people do when the BTC begins to infect their neighborhood. They move. So that's what I did. I gave up on the city of Cleveland, my home for three decades, and moved to the suburbs.

No big deal, you say. Everybody moves sometime, you say. But if you look at the cover of this book, that is my grandma's house in 2015, just before they tore it down because it was a condemned property. Not a pretty sight, eh? When my family owned the house for over 50 years we always paid the property taxes that supported our local school system. And everyone in my family who lived there worked and paid other taxes.

After I moved out of the neighborhood it became a Section 8 neighborhood which I will explain in a few more pages. Eventually the old Jedick family home was condemned and torn down. So there went another chunk of tax dollars. No more property taxes. No more residents paying other taxes.

The city of Cleveland and its school system just became a bit poorer. Multiply that scenario by the thousands of other condemned buildings and empty lots in the city of Cleveland and you can see why the city of Cleveland tanked. That is why there are now two kinds of neighborhoods in the city of Cleveland, white neighborhoods and BSC neighborhoods.

Actually, the smart white people started moving out of Cleveland way back in 1966, after Carl Stokes was elected the first black mayor of a major American city. They could see the writing on the wall. Cleveland's population dropped from 876,000 in 1960 to 750,903 by the end of the decade. That is a downward trend that continues to this day. Meanwhile its black population doubled between 1950 and 1965, from 147,847 to 279,352. But more importantly the city also lost 80,000 jobs in the 1960s. The BSC was chasing small businesses out of the neighborhoods but you never read about that in the history books. Instead Carl Stokes is portrayed by the media as a hero. There are so many buildings and streets named after Stokes in Cleveland it will make your head spin.

Stokes himself gave a frank description of the city's problems in a 1968 speech that was quoted in the book *Where the River Burned* by Richard and David Stradling.

Stokes told a Washington D.C. crowd that Cleveland had "spreading slums, increasing crime, declining tax duplicate, (rising) infant mortality and illiteracy rates, air and water pollution, and the mounting tensions between the races." I doubt if he blamed the BSC for any of it.

Back to my grandma's house in 1982. My two young children were approaching school age and at the time there was something going on in the city of Cleveland called "Forced School Busing for Racial Integration." (We will explore school busing in another chapter.) White kids from my neighborhood were being bused to black neighborhoods where they could learn how to act like black thugs at an early age. (SSDAS)

We lived very close to a public elementary school. It was a blessing to my grandmother as she raised her six children. But thanks to school busing it turned into a curse for my family.

Every morning yellow school buses drove down our street and dropped black kids off at the school. Some of them went inside the school while others skipped school and ran around the neighborhood all day. Suddenly items began to go missing from my neighbors' garages.

There went the neighborhood.

I did not want the BTC infecting my children with its lifestyle. So we did what any concerned parents would do. We sold our house. I did not want to move to the suburbs, the same suburbs that I had mocked my whole life as a native Clevelander, but we had to do it. So much for all the sweat equity I had put into the house.

That's why I call it the "Black Thug Culture" (BTC) as opposed the "Black Subculture" (BSC). The young kids across the street were well on their way to becoming the black thugs of the future. They probably ended up in jail sometime in their lifetime because that's what the statistics predict will happen to them.

It is not their fault. It is the government system that created them and their environment in the first place. It is why our nation is on the verge of bankruptcy. Let me explain my theory in simple terms that I hope you can understand.

In order to understand why the United States of America is on the verge of bankruptcy you must first understand what has happened to our tax base. And one of the easiest ways to comprehend what has happened to our country over the last 50 years is to look at our neighborhoods.

We can use the city of Cleveland's neighborhoods as an example. This is where the taxes come from to pay for what we expect our government to provide for us. Services like police, fire, schools, roads and garbage pickup on a local level. And our country's defense on the national level.

But in the last 50 years our government has grown by leaps and bounds, offering services never dreamed about by our Founding Fathers. Yet the neighborhoods that pay for them are shedding taxpayers by the millions.

Listen, my friends, and you shall hear, about all the factors that put us here. Let's start with one of the key ones, Section 8 housing.

To understand what happened to many of the neighborhoods in our big cities you have to understand what Section 8 housing is all about. Yet when I question many of my white suburban friends about it, they are completely clueless. They never heard of it. Just like the many Americans who live in small towns, it has never affected them. So they have no knowledge of its existence or how it is draining our treasury of billions of dollars every year, in direct and indirect ways.

Let's start with the term "There Goes The Neighborhood." Where does that saying come from? In my lifetime it was used by white people when blacks moved into their neighborhood.

But, you ask, why should that be such a problem? What about all the other nationalities that live in a city like my home town, Cleveland, Ohio? Wasn't Cleveland once famous as a melting pot of cultures? Aren't blacks just another ethnic group among many? Oh how I wish that were so, my naïve friend. African Americans quit being like all our other minorities once they became the only official "government approved minority."

Somewhere around the 1960s black leaders convinced Democratic politicians that their people should receive special treatment to make up for their being slaves a hundred years earlier. No matter that my grand-father working in a coal mine had it just as tough as a black guy working in a cotton field.

The politicians bought the argument and started giving black people all kinds of free stuff in exchange for their vote. The squeaky wheel gets the grease.

In order to understand how the United States of America was trans-formed from the richest country in the world into one up to its armpits in debt, you must first understand what happened to all of our great cities. Cities like Cleveland and Detroit are on the cutting edge of what is happening all across our great land. Let's examine Cleveland, my home town, to show you what I am talking about.

The city of Cleveland is now about 53 percent African American. It is in danger of becoming another Detroit, Michigan, which just went through bankruptcy proceedings, the wave of the future. One of the first things you must understand about the BSC is that even when blacks are in the majority, when they become the largest ethnic group in the city, many still want all kinds of special treatment as a "minority."

This is where the Black Subculture comes into play. It is what makes the BSC so different from true minorities like Eskimos or Taiwanese.

I know what you might be thinking, especially if you are a Democrat or a black person reading this. This guy must be a racist for even suggesting such things. I completely understand where you are coming from.

So before I proceed let me make my views perfectly clear. If a nice black family moves into my neighborhood I don't have a problem with that. Let's say President Obama and Michele move in. They seem like a nice couple who take care of their kids. I don't know if they know much about taking care of their own property since they've been living off the taxpayers for a great chunk of their married life but I'll give them a pass on that one.

"Welcome to the neighborhood," I'd say. But that is not the way it works in our big cities. Instead of a nice nuclear family like the Obamas moving in, our new neighbors would probably be a single mom on welfare who is overwhelmed with a handful of young children that she cannot control because she expects the government to take care of them for her. So her kids partner up with other welfare children and end up terrorizing their new neighborhood.

"There goes the neighborhood," anyone?

The nuclear black family is practically nonexistent thanks to the policies of our federal government that reward unwed black women for having babies. You can hear the same argument from black citizens also.

The May 27, 2015 *Plain Dealer* was almost totally dedicated to a new U. S. Department of Justice settlement with the Cleveland Police Department about police department reforms. But columnist Mark Naymik added a comment from a 59-year-old black roofer whom he met at a community forum, who stated that the reforms would be useless unless black youth were taught respect for the police.

"A lack of male leadership is the problem," he said. ... "There are too few black men willing and able to show the way."

The blacks who began moving into old Cleveland neighborhoods like mine were nothing like the strong nuclear white families that I knew growing up and going to school in the city of Cleveland.

What the feds do is subsidize a black underclass where the kids are out of control, crime is rampant and the schools are dysfunctional. It is the source of all the problems plaguing our big cities today.

It all began with a federal government program called "Aid to Families with Dependent Children" (ADFC) or more simply "Aid to Dependent Children" (ADC). It was started with good intentions like most government programs. Way back in 1935 it was a part of the Social Security Act called "Mother's Aid," and it was supposed to help poor children without fathers during the Great Depression.

The idea was to help children whose fathers died, became incapacitated or deserted their family. But the black community hijacked the program. They quickly discovered that if you had a child out of wedlock the government would throw you some cash. The more children the more cash. And you would also qualify for lots of other free stuff. It is a lot easier than working for a living.

So young unwed women can begin receiving government benefits as soon as they have a baby. That is, as long as the baby does not have a father. Who comes up with these crazy ideas? And why weren't they stopped when the results became obvious?

Actually by 1996 Americans realized that our welfare system was out of control. They saw that there was a 27 percent rise in ADC caseloads from 1990 to 1994. So the Republican Congress led by Newt Gingrich and Bob Dole tried to fix the broken system in 1996 when it passed a welfare reform bill called "The Personal Responsibility and Work Opportunity Reconciliation Act." President Bill Clinton vetoed it twice before finally signing it with an election coming. Then he took credit for it.

It replaced ADC with TANF, "Temporary Assistance for Needy Families." TANF gave more responsibility to the states for administering welfare through block grants. Each state came up with its own formulas but they still dished out lots of free stuff.

Unfortunately, the tradition of unwed moms was already ingrained in the inner city BSC. So fathers are still few and far between in inner city black families. If you don't believe me just listen to the radio commercials the government uses to promote fatherhood. They are sponsored by the U.S. Department of Health and Human Services, the same bureaucracy that spent $17 billion in 2014 giving away free stuff to the moms without husbands. Whenever I hear one these commercials I just shake my head. I ask myself, why do we even need these?

Simple. It is because the federal government has created an entire subculture of single women on welfare. Who comes up with these crazy ideas? The Democratic Party, that's who, beginning with President Kennedy and his group of Ivy League advisors, "the best and the brightest." After he was assassinated, Lyndon B. Johnson used his political acumen to put their ideas into law.

The Democratic Party soon discovered that if they provide the BSC with lots of free stuff they can count on their automatic vote for the rest of their lifetime. They offered black women a free place to live in exchange for their loyalty. But if they have a husband they don't qualify for all the free stuff.

So there is no one to help these young black women maintain their property or take care of their children. They expect the government to do it for them. This is the policy that created the "black thugs." There are millions of them running the streets of our nation and sitting in our prisons. Crime runs rampant in the BSC neighborhoods because young black males have no adult male mentors. There are horrific examples of it every day in our daily newspapers. Citizens are robbed and killed just walking down the street in the BSC neighborhoods. Businesses close down or move. No one pays any taxes. It becomes a downward spiral that never stops.

Later I'll show you the details of this phenomenon when we examine the classic BSC Cleveland suburb, East Cleveland, a 99 percent black community that cannot pay its bills. It is a miniature version of the once great city of Detroit.

But for now let us return to our discussion of Section 8 housing. Fortunately most Americans have never experienced it. But their tax money is supporting it and it is slowly destroying our country, neighborhood by neighborhood. It is also why our country is going bankrupt.

Someday it will be in your neighborhood also. It is just a matter of time. In fact, it probably already is in your neighborhood, you just aren't aware of it. I have suggested in the past that any property paid for by Section 8 should be required to have a sign in its front yard that says: "Thank you, taxpayers, for paying my Section 8 rent." Then our citizens would know how much Section 8 housing is actually out there.

Section 8 has slowly expanded from big cities like Cleveland and Detroit into what are now called "inner ring suburbs." From there it moves out into the "outer ring suburbs." Eventually the outer ring suburbs will expand from one city to the next, like from Cleveland to Akron and Youngstown.

It is just a matter of time before it is everywhere.

Don't believe me? Let's take a look at my grandmother's old neighborhood today, thirty years later.

My grandmother's neighborhood is now filled with Section 8 housing. It has become one of the most dangerous neighborhoods in the city. The homicide rate is through the roof.

Why? Because the BSC expanded across the Cuyahoga River from the east side to the west side. The east side of Cleveland is now almost completely black. It has more empty lots and abandoned houses than the city knows what to do with.

The federal government believes it is its duty to help poor blacks move out of their crime-ridden neighborhoods and into the nicer neighborhoods. (They are never held responsible for the destruction of their own neighborhoods in the first place.)

Notice this only applies to blacks. Other ethnic groups are on their own. If this isn't a racist policy I don't know what is. Why is this government help only offered to blacks? Because other blacks administer the program. (More on this later when we discuss middle class blacks.)

All they have to do is sign up for the Section 8 rent subsidies. If they qualify it is like hitting the lottery. This gives them a method by which they can upgrade their living conditions without using any "sweat equity" of their own. They can live in any rental property that accepts Section 8 vouchers. Thank you BSC.

Every house I ever moved into was totally upgraded before I moved out. The same can be said for the homes of most of my friends and relatives. How many black Section 8 renters can say that? Very few, I assure you.

Enough details about Section 8, I hope I didn't overwhelm you. Let us fast forward to August 13, 2012, about 30 years after I moved out of Cleveland. I am working as a Cleveland fireman two neighborhoods further west than my grandmother's. It is still predominantly white but begin-ning to flip.

An elderly woman, who reminds me of my grandmother, asks us, the Cleveland Fire Department, to replace her smoke detectors. It is a free service that we do for the city's residents.

As we replace the smoke detectors I ask her how long she's lived in her modest house and how she likes living there. She has lived there for a very long time, over 50 years, just like my grandmother. Her house and yard are immaculate, just like my grandmother kept hers.

"But the blacks are moving in," she tells me. "Blacks don't want to move in, they want to take over."

She has hit the nail on its head. This is the difference between the BSC and Cleveland's other ethnic groups. She tells me there have been a lot of break-ins on Bosworth Avenue, a main street near her home with lots of small apartment buildings, magnets for Section 8 housing. She is begin-ning to fear for her safety.

"We're thinking about moving to the suburbs," she says. I don't have the heart to tell her but it is too late for her to move. Thanks to the influx of Section 8 blacks into her neighborhood, her house is now basically worthless.

(Please pay close attention here, my trusted readers, because this is another very important effect the BSC has on our city's welfare. It causes property values to plummet which in turn dries up the tax income our cities need to survive.)

Despite paying taxes for decades and keeping her property immacu-late, inside and out, she and her husband are destined to live out the remainder of their lives as virtual prisoners in their own home. As the BSC presence grows, it will become increasingly dangerous for them to leave their house.

This is the real tragedy of Section 8 housing. It is what "subsidized" or

Section 8 housing is really all about. It is the great American tragedy and no one in the media or academia is even addressing the issue. (SSDAS)

For decades the U.S. government took this hard-working white family's tax money and gave it to welfare-addicted black families so they could live anywhere they wanted, even the nicest neighborhoods in the city and its suburbs. As long as the federal government provides this crutch, many blacks don't have to earn that privilege like white people do. That's why the old white people would say: "There Goes the Neighborhood" when Section 8 black families moved in.

Section 8 subsidized housing is administered by the Cuyahoga Metropolitan Housing Authority (CMHA). It is named after the county Cleveland is located in. There are very few white people working for the CMHA. (SSDAS) It is black people giving away white people's money to their fellow blacks. It is a racist system perpetuated by the Democratic Party to buy the votes of black voters.

That is the system that was created in the United States of America by two Democratic presidents: John F. Kennedy and Lyndon B. Johnson, a couple darlings of the media. Their "Great Society" doesn't look so great up close and personal, especially if you are a taxpayer, white or black.

The government has thrown billions of dollars at the problem for five decades. And what are the results? Inner city black populations are just as poor as ever and according to the government's own statistics, poverty rates among all the population are higher than ever. (SSDAS) (See my chapter on how we lost The War on Poverty.)

The day before I spoke with the elderly white lady there was an article in the Cleveland *Plain Dealer* about a black civic activist who was complaining about the conditions of her apartment. She was paying $82 a month for her $1000 a month apartment thanks to subsidized housing. And she's been living in it most of her life. The media completely missed the irony there. Instead of screaming "discrimination" the black lady should be thanking the white lady we visited for paying her rent for her throughout most of her lifetime. Like that's going to happen.

And on the same day the city swimming pool in the white lady's neighborhood was forced to close two weeks before summer vacation ended. Why? Because the city of Cleveland could not afford to keep it open.

Why are the city of Cleveland's residents some of the poorest in the country? Have you been paying attention? If not, let me repeat my premise one more time.

The city of Cleveland has changed from a melting pot to an ink pot. It is now a black majority city and the BSC doesn't pay taxes. Instead they demand and receive expensive services that they cannot afford. They just expect the white taxpayers to keep paying for them.

And why is this policy bankrupting our entire country? Are we not a rich nation that can afford to help our poorest citizens? We once were but are not anymore. We are up to our ears in debt.

Taking care of the BSC costs us millions of dollars a day in a variety of ways, everything from administering food stamps to building and maintaining prisons. The problem is that the federal government keeps creating a larger and larger BSC footprint. Young black women follow in their mothers' footsteps. They learn from their example. We are running out of working white families to pay for all the free stuff the Democrats promised the black families. "The Great Society" is coming back to bite us on our butts.

So what is the city of Cleveland's solution to the dilemma it finds itself in? It wants to borrow millions of dollars from the State of Ohio and the federal government to tear down all the condemned properties like my grandma's house that were ruined by the BSC.

In fact, that is my grandmother's house on the cover of this book. They tore it down just as I finished writing this. There was nothing physically wrong with it. It could have been remodeled again like I did if someone wanted to move into that neighborhood. But there aren't any takers.

So what does it all mean? It means that there goes one more chunk of the city of Cleveland's tax base. Multiply that a couple thousand times and you can see why our big cities are all in financial trouble. This is not a solution but at least it helps remove the problem properties that attract criminals and vagrants from the neighborhoods.

Eventually, the once stable west side of Cleveland is going to begin looking like its east side which today resembles the old newsreels of Germany after World War II. Whole sections of Cleveland's east side have nothing but empty streets and abandoned houses and businesses. I know because I watched a lot of them burn down.

Why do I think this is going to also happen to the west side? Because once too many black thugs move into a neighborhood it begins to re-segregate itself. It flips from white to black. And if there is one thing I know from my many years on this planet it is that I have yet to meet a white person who wants to move into a BSC neighborhood. Blacks, on the other hand, love to move into a stable white neighborhood. Isn't it obvious why that is? Just something to ponder as we head into our next chapter.

So let us now take a closer look at President Lyndon Johnson's "War on Poverty" on its 50th Anniversary.

Spoiler Alert: We lost.

CHAPTER SIX:
THE WAR ON POVERTY (WHY WE LOST)

"When what you're doing doesn't work for 50 years, it's time to try something new."—President Barack Obama, State of the Union Address, January 20, 2015

WE LEFT OFF last chapter delving into the effects of President Lyndon B. Johnson's "War on Poverty." I was summarizing my belief that the war actually had the opposite effect than the one intended. I wanted to prove to you that we lost this war for the same reasons that we lost the war in Vietnam. We did not use the right tactics.

We lost in Vietnam because we did not understand jungle warfare. We lost the "war on poverty" in our nation's big cities because we did not understand the BSC. Johnson's failed "war on poverty" is the main reason we have a race problem in the twenty-first century United States of America. We need to explore the Black Subculture in our country and understand how it resembles the Communist society of the Soviet Union during the cold war.

By that I mean the BSC is almost totally dependent on the government for its survival. Many Americans do not realize that without economic freedom political freedom is meaningless.

As I was searching for a way to convince you of my views without overloading you with facts and figures I stumbled upon an op-ed column written by *New York Times* columnist Nicholas Kristof titled: "When Liberals Blew It."

The date was March 12, 2015 and Kristof was telling the story of the famous "Moynihan Report" written 50 years ago. Daniel Patrick Moynihan's 1965 report was titled "The Negro Family: The Case for National Action." And he said it caused a national furor.

When I read his column I almost yelled "Eureka!" It was like finding a pot of gold in my backyard a few days before St. Patrick's Day and a week before President Obama planned to visit my home town of Cleveland, Ohio.

What an eye opener. Here is someone who was preaching the same Gospel as myself 50 years ago. And he was even a high ranking Democrat. Daniel Patrick Moynihan was an Assistant Secretary of Labor in President Lyndon B. Johnson's cabinet.

Kristof begins his article with a bold statement:

"Fifty years ago this month Democrats made a historic mistake."
"Daniel Patrick Moynihan, at the time a Federal official, wrote a famous report in March 1965 on family breakdown among African Americans. He argued presciently and powerfully that the rise of single-parent households would make poverty more intractable."

Amen, to that brother.
Kristof goes on to further explain Moynihan's views:

"The fundamental problem, Moynihan wrote, is family breakdown."

Then Kristof took this quote from a follow-up report Moynihan wrote for the Jesuit magazine, *America*:

"From the wild Irish slums of the 19th-century Eastern seaboard, to the riot-torn suburbs of Los Angeles, there is one unmistakable lesson in American history: a community that allows large numbers of young men to grow up in broken families ... never acquiring any stable relationship to male authority, never acquiring any set of rational expectations about the future—that community asks for and gets chaos. Crime, violence, unrest, disorder ... are not only to be expected, they are very near to inevitable. And they are richly deserved."

You would think that Moynihan would have been applauded for creating such a detailed expose of such a major American problem. Wrong again, Kemosabe. Instead the black leaders of the day practically crucified him for daring to broach the subject.

Here is what Kristof said about the reaction of Democratic politicians, black leaders and the media.

"Liberals brutally denounced Moynihan as a racist. He himself had grown up in a single-mother household and worked as a shoeshine boy at the corner of Broadway and 43rd Street in Manhattan, yet he was accused of being aloof and patronizing, and of 'blaming the victim.'"

"The liberal denunciations of Moynihan were terribly unfair," Kristof concluded. "Scholars, fearful of being accused of racism, mostly avoided studying family structure and poverty."

In other words, the main subject of this book, that the lack of black fathers in the BSC are at the root of most of today's social problems, became a "no-no" for a generation of liberal thinkers and America was well on the road to bankruptcy.

What did Moynihan do that was so terribly wrong? He simply presented an accurate view of the BSC culture, complete with graphs and charts to back up his arguments.

So what did we end up with for the past 50 years? An explosion of the "Black Subculture." Thank you one more time, my fellow Democrats.

To really appreciate Moynihan's groundbreaking report you have to read it in its entirety. Prepare to be amazed. It is a very long and very comprehensive.

And to help you make sense of it you also have to read a July 31, 1966, New York Times article by Thomas Meehan titled "Moynihan of the Moynihan Report." He does a great job of dissecting Moynihan's views and the reaction to them.

The third section of my book is titled "Voices in the Wilderness." There I highlight certain sections from the actual Moynihan Report that apply to my simple thesis that the Black Subculture needs to be dismantled from the inside out.

If you want to read his entire report and the entire Meehan article about it you can find links to both of them at my web site: www.peterjedick.com.

Now let's get back to what happened after the Moynihan Report was issued. Did President Johnson declare a "War on Poverty," that championed nuclear Negro families and everyone lived happily ever after? Oh how I wish it were true.

Instead the federal government did what it always does. It threw money at "the poverty problem." It spent billions upon billions of dollars setting up new government programs. And what did it accomplish with all that money? Let me just say this before we look at the results of our 50 year "War on Poverty."

It would have been a lot easier and cheaper to just give everyone in America a cash bonus. Here are the sad results of our 50 year "War on Poverty" according to Kristof's article:

"In 2013, 71 percent of black children in America were born to an unwed mother, as were 53 percent of Hispanic children and 36 percent of white children.

"Indeed the single parent is the new norm. At some point before they turn 18, a majority of all U.S. children will likely live with a single mom and no dad. ... Partly because there is often only one income coming into a single-parent household, children of unmarried moms are roughly five times more likely to live in poverty as children of married couples."

In other words, the BSC lifestyle is a virus that has exploded across the American landscape. It is now infecting our entire country, growing larger every day. We need a national policy to address this issue but I do not see one on the horizon. Who is even talking about it?

Nicholas Kristof created a fine piece of journalism. I humbly bow down to his brave declarations. However, like everyone else in the media, he stops short of supplying a real solution to the racial dilemma we find in twenty-first Century America. Just like the scholars he chastised, he is probably afraid of being branded a racist. So he doesn't go far enough.

His solution is to support programs to help young women delay child-bearing. Of course, I agree with him. That is the whole idea of this book. How many times have I mentioned, my patient readers, that what we need is to stop paying unwed young women to have babies. But it is not going to happen with any new government programs. Instead we need to eliminate the ones that we already have on the books.

What we need to do is to stop subsidizing unwed moms right here and now. I am not proposing we throw these young mothers out on the street. If they are fortunate enough to already be in the program they can keep sucking it dry. But let us put a stop to it right here and now. Pick a date and put the word out on the streets that the federal and state governments will no longer provide unwed moms with the free baby shower package that is now available.

When I addressed the young crowd at Oberlin College years ago I was more compassionate. I realized that anyone can make a mistake and maybe we could subsidize one out-of-wedlock child per mother. Then, once they learned their lesson, draw the line there.

But since then we've added trillions of dollars to our national debt. We can no longer afford to be so generous.

We have to tell every teenager in America that too many unwed moms have abused the system for over half a century and it is dead broke. No more free stuff for unwed moms. If you want to start a family you'd better make sure you have a father and a mother and one of you has a job and medical benefits. It worked in America for 200 years and it can work again.

The word on the streets will spread quickly, I guarantee it. The feminists will scream bloody murder but who cares? Once we do it, the United States of America will make an historic turnaround. I rest my case.

Well, I almost rested my case. Just about the time I finished writing this chapter another incident happened in our fair country that underscores what I have been saying.

On Monday, April 27, 2015, blacks rioted in Baltimore, Maryland, because a black guy named Freddie Gray was supposedly killed by police brutality. Whether that is true or not I will let the courts decide. However, the Associated Press story about the Baltimore neighborhood where the rioting occurred is right out of my text.

Here are some paragraphs lifted from the story by Associated Press reporters Amanda Lee Myers and David Dishneau in my April 29, 2015 *Plain Dealer*.

"Monday's outbreak of looting, arson and rock throwing by mostly black rioters erupted just hours after Gray's funeral. It was the worst such violence in the U.S. since the unrest last year over the death of Michael Brown."

"Some of the same neighborhoods that rose up this week burned for days after the assassination of the Rev. Martin Luther King 47 years ago. At least six people died then, and some neighborhoods still bear the scars."

"They aren't protesting. They aren't making a statement. They're stealing," Obama said.

"At least 20 officers were hurt, one person was critically injured in a fire, more than 200 adults and 34 juveniles were arrested, and nearly 150 cars were burned, police said."

"The violence set off soul searching by community leaders ... suggesting ... it was about high unemployment, high crime, poor housing, broken-down schools and lack of opportunity in Baltimore's inner-city neighborhoods."

"The city of 622,000 is 63 percent black. The mayor, state's attorney, police chief and City Council president are black, as is 48 percent of the police force."

So once again: How's this "War on Poverty" working for the city of Baltimore? Think many businesses are planning on moving into any of its riot-torn neighborhoods? Think its property values are going to go up or down for the next few years?

Baltimore, Cleveland, Detroit, Chicago, Los Angeles. The Black Subculture is a national problem. And we need new solutions to fix it.

I rest my case one more time.

CHAPTER SEVEN:
WHERE DO OUR TAXES GO

"The top 20 percent of taxpayers—those earning $134,300 or more—account for about 84 percent of all federal tax revenue."— THE WEEK MAGAZINE, April 24, 2015 issue

THAT'S ABOUT WHAT most state governors are paid. And they have the awesome responsibility of overseeing billion-dollar budgets. It is also about what our astronauts are paid for spending years preparing to go into outer space.

So much for knocking the "one percenters." Let's give a cheer for the "twenty percenters."

Here's my gripe about our tax system. I've been paying taxes since I was 16 years old and I don't mind one single bit.

My first job was packing bags for the cashiers at our local A&P grocery store. It was harder than it sounds. We only had paper bags back then and the manager frowned on us using double bags because a paper bag cost two cents each. That hurt his bottom line. But if a customer broke a bag on their way to their car and spilled peaches all over the parking lot they might not come back. There was a real art to packing those bags correctly.

I also learned to mop the floor and deal with the public, two tasks that would help me with some of my later careers. And it made me a self-starter. I can still remember the manager yelling at us during a slow period: "I'm not paying you guys $2 an hour to stand around with your thumbs up your butts. Find something to do or I'll find someone to replace you."

Immediately, all the baggers started running around straightening cans or bringing in shopping carts from the parking lot.

It was a challenging profession but I learned a lot. I learned to punch a time card. If you punched in over eight minutes late you were docked a quarter hour. Same thing for your lunch hour and two fifteen minute breaks. The time clock ruled my life.

Still, I figured I was going to be the richest kid in my neighborhood because I was pulling down $2 an hour. Or so I thought. I remember looking at my first paycheck and asking my dad what the deductions were all about. He told me to get used to it.

The "War on Poverty" was just beginning and I was a foot soldier. They took out for city, state and federal taxes, Social Security, Medicare, Medicaid and union dues. My $2 an hour didn't seem so much anymore. That's how my job history began and over the years I held more jobs than I can even remember. The deductions went on more or less the same for the next half century.

But I didn't really care that much. The way I looked at it I led a pretty comfortable life here in the United States of America. I've always had a roof over my head and a refrigerator filled with food. I can jump in my car and drive wherever I want without a policeman following me. I can even write a book like this criticizing the government and not be sent to Siberia for my beliefs. I can own a gun to protect myself. I can even go to downtown Cleveland, stand on a soapbox in the middle of Public Square and scream that President Obama is a loser without being arrested.

I could go on and on but I think you catch my drift. We have economic and political freedoms that most people in the world would die for. In fact, a lot of our citizens throughout our history did just that, they died to protect our freedoms.

That is the price we pay to be Americans. So it always kind of bothered me that cheating on our taxes is almost a national pastime. We need to pay taxes so our Armed Forces can protect us from our enemies. Aircraft carriers, nuclear submarines and jet bombers don't come cheap. We need the government to build our roads, bridges and airports. They have to pick up our garbage and clear the snow off our highways. If I am robbed I can call for the police and they show up. Someone has to pay the cops. The same goes for the firemen. I need them if I have a heart attack or my house catches on fire. And fire engines don't come cheap either.

I am always amazed that when I turn my faucet on clean drinking water comes out of it. Most Americans do not appreciate what a luxury that is in many parts of the world. I appreciate everything there is about being an American citizen.

However, the time has come to have a conversation about what we expect from our government and what we do not need. We need to take a close look at where our tax money goes and set some new priorities.

Let me use my own personal taxes as an example. I live a nice middle class lifestyle. I own my own home. (Well, actually the bank owns my home, but it lets me live here as long as I make my monthly payment.) I make pretty good money but I am by no means a one percenter, not even a twenty percenter. I've been trying to crack the six figure income bracket all my life to no avail.

Yet I paid almost $13,000 in federal taxes in 2014. I paid the state of Ohio almost $3,000. And I paid the local tax agency $2300 that was split between the suburb where I live and the city of Cleveland where I worked. I also paid taxes for Social Security, Medicare, Medicaid and property taxes to fund the local public schools that I don't send my kids to.

Like I said I do not mind paying the taxes. I would just like a breakdown as to where the money goes. First of all, how much of my federal taxes now goes to pay the interest on our national debt. How much of it is given to foreign dictators in the name of "foreign aid"? How much of it goes to fund the Department of Health and Human Services which takes my taxes and gives it to people who don't work?

Every American taxpayer needs to ask these same questions. According to my May 1, 2015 copy of *The Week Magazine*: "Americans paid more income tax in raw dollars in 2014 than ever before. The Office of Management and Budget estimates that $1.4 trillion was turned over in income tax last year, or around $4,400 per person."

That sounds to me like a lot of money. But $1.4 TRILLION doesn't amount to a hill of beans when we are over $18 trillion in debt and our debt is growing by over $2 billion every day.

Our $1.4 trillion is barely enough to pay what we already owe China and Japan. When is this nonsense going to end? How will we ever pay off that $18 trillion? Does anyone in Washington really care?

That is why all Americans should be very upset with their federal government. My question is how much of my tax money has gone to support the chronically unemployable throughout my lifetime? (SSDAS) What does it cost to support one welfare mother with three kids and no husband nowadays? How much does her family receive for a year in TANF payments, food stamps, rent subsidies, free medical care and all the rest?

And then what about her offspring? As I speculated in my "Introduction" chapter, what if one unwed teenage mom had a child and went directly on welfare the same year I started paying taxes? Then she had a couple other babies before she was twenty. If her three children followed her example and reproduced as teenagers themselves by the time they were 20 and then their three kids followed suit etc. and etc. the original mom could be a great grandmother by the time I retired. And I could be supporting 39 of her offspring, besides the original mom, in my lifetime.

And that is only if each child only has three children of her own. Most unwed moms have more than three because the more they have the more free stuff the government throws at them.

So my $13,000 a year in taxes comes up way short in the welfare child support lottery. In other words for the last 50 years I've been working to support two families, my own and one that I have never met.

My BIG question is this: Is any of my tax money left over to help pay for the basic government services we all need to survive as a country?

I have a feeling that all my hard-earned tax money is not even enough to support one unwed welfare family almost equal to my own. How many taxpayers does it take to support the entire BSC?

And even more importantly, how much does the BSC pay in taxes? Giving some of your welfare money back to the government that gave it to you in the first place does not add anything to our country's wealth. (SSDAS)

Even President Obama, who paid $93,362 in federal taxes on $477,383 of income in 2014, is merely giving back to the taxpayers some of the money they gave him in the first place.

The way I look at it the BSC is not paying its fair share for the privilege of living in America. I don't have the numbers. Someone should do a study. (SSDAS) But I feel in my gut that our nation has long ago passed the tipping point where there are not enough of us working to support those of us not working.

Is it any wonder our country is bankrupt? No wonder we have to borrow billions of dollars every day to keep our government functioning. No wonder we don't have enough left over to support our military.

I heard a figure bantered about on the radio that 92 million Americans don't work. I don't know if that includes children and retired seniors but that's a lot of people on the dole out of 320 million Americans.

Something has to give. Something has to change and change soon or we are on the road to our own destruction. Actually we already are.

We didn't have the U.S. Department of Housing and Urban Development (HUD) when I was growing up and we got along just fine. It was created in 1965 as another part of President Lyndon Johnson's "Great Society."

Then by the time I moved out on my own in the late 1970s not only was the Section 8 program invented (we discussed this earlier) but our local Cuyahoga Metropolitan Housing Authority (CMHA) expanded into something called the "scattered site housing program."

The CMHA actually bought three houses on my father's street and six other houses nearby. Then they rented them at a discount to "low income families" all of whom happened to be black. And they did the same thing throughout the west side of Cleveland. Today CMHA owns about 500 such "scattered site" houses for their low income clients.

What is a government agency doing owning houses? That smells like communism under the Russians in the Cold War. If the government owns your house they have complete control over your lifestyle. That is why Fannie Mae and Freddie Mac need to be put out of business. Americans do not realize how many of our mortgages they control. If they did I am sure they would be upset about it.

What happened in my father's neighborhood was not very different than the forced busing experiment. Except instead of federal judges forcing integration in our schools, government bureaucrats were forcing integration in our neighborhoods. The head of the CMHA was wielding more power than our duly elected mayor. What's up with that?

My father already lived next to one of the largest public housing complexes in the city, which I discussed earlier, and it was also beginning to turn black.

Once again the "government approved minority," African Americans, were enjoying a free upgrade. Instead of working their way from their inner city neighborhoods to the outer city limits like my dad did, many black families were practically given a free house in a nice neighborhood compliments of CMHA.

At first, my dad and mom welcomed the new black families into our neighborhood. They seemed like nice people. But then their friends from the BTC began to visit them and the situation began to deteriorate.

Suddenly it was no longer possible for neighborhood kids to leave their bikes on their front lawn overnight. They would disappear. When I stopped over to visit them I could not go up to our corner store without a black dude trying to sell me some crack. When I walked my dad's dog past the corner bus stop a black chick propositioned me.

My childhood neighborhood was changing from Mayberry to Watts right in front of my eyes. And as typically happens, the corner store soon went out of business, the same one that was a neighborhood staple throughout my childhood.

There goes the tax base. There goes the neighborhood. Thank you, CMHA and HUD, for using our own hard-earned tax dollars to ruin our own neighborhood.

What is their budget every year? HUD asked for $56 billion, not million, but billion dollars in 2015 to help them administer such programs as public housing. And what happened to our public housing developments, "the projects" that are scattered around our fair city?

Today they are mostly crime-ridden, drug-infested slums. That was what they were supposed to replace in the first place. That is why the CMHA invented the "scattered site" housing program. To give its "clients" a chance to move out of the projects that the CMHA had trashed in the first place.

Where will this all end? How many soldiers could we give a raise with $56 billion? How many ships could we build for our navy?

So what have our two government agencies accomplished since 1965? The sad fact is that neither CMHA nor HUD care much about housing maintenance. Too boring. Most of the public housing complexes that they fund are falling into disrepair. They are a haven for criminals like drug dealers and car thieves. Like I said, isn't this what they were created to replace?

It is time for us to decide: what is the function of our government? Is it to give away free stuff from cradle to grave? There is a government housing project on Cleveland's east side that recently named one of its streets after an elderly resident who has lived there all her life. Why is that something to celebrate? Shouldn't she be ashamed of herself? No, that is the BSC mindset.

In Part Two of this book I will explain in detail the Black Subculture to those who have no clue about what it is. But before we can change our BSC into a Black Prosperous Culture we are going to need a new tax system. One that encourages our entire economy to grow and prosper instead of dragging it down.

Payroll taxes do not work. There are way too many deductions and loopholes. It is too easy to cheat the government. And that does not even count all the millions that the IRS gives away every year to identity thieves.

In a March 12, 2015 article on tax ID fraud *Plain Dealer* reporter Teresa Dixon Murray stated: "From early 2011 through October 2014, the IRS paid 5.2 BILLION [my caps] in income tax refunds that were later determined to stem from identity theft fraud."

No wonder our country is broke. Who are these people and what happens to them when we catch them? Do we ever catch them?

Here's more from the same article: "According to [Ohio Senator Sherrod] Brown's office, the IRS estimated it prevented 19 million cases of fraudulent identity theft returns worth more than $63 BILLION [my caps] between 2011 and 2014."

Does this make any sense to anyone out there? Nineteen million cases of identity theft returns were caught? How many weren't caught? Once again who are these people and why can't we put them all in jail? It is time to come up with a new tax system pronto. A system that cannot be gamed by the house, i.e. the government.

This all has to stop and stop right now.

There is a movement afoot to overhaul our tax system and I am all for it.

Some people are proposing a national sales tax to replace our payroll tax. The nice thing about this system is that everybody pays no matter what your income. Everyone is in. I like that. We should all contribute to the welfare of our country. And it does not stifle one's desire to make more money for your family.

Others argue for a flat payroll tax with no deductions. I like that idea also. Everyone pays the same whether you are receiving welfare or a millionaire. Of course, the welfare recipient is just giving the government back some of its own money. But the way it works now the tax brackets system destroys any incentive to work harder.

Maybe we can do a combination of both ideas.

I've worked at least two jobs most of my life. But if I've learned one thing it is that the more you make, the more the IRS takes. Sometimes you wonder if it is worth the effort to even get up in the morning. It's like the Beatles song, "Taxman."

We need to simplify our tax structure.

Here's an idea I would like to put out there. We can build upon it. Maybe something to kick start a debate about our tax system. What if everyone in America pays 10 percent to the feds, two percent to our state and one percent to our local government. No more deductions for anyone or anything. We merely tell our governments that this is what they have to live on. If it doesn't work we can adjust the percentages accordingly. Their main job is to protect our democratic way of life from our enemies and I want to make sure we have enough funds to do the job properly.

But there is one big problem with reforming our archaic tax code. What do we do with all the accountants who make their living filling out these complex forms? I like my tax guys. They are nice people with nice families. I'd hate to see them lose their jobs. Any change has consequences with our economy.

So here's my idea. Since we have all these problems with identity theft let us use our accountants as a private buffer for our tax returns.

Make them all register with the government and then the IRS tells our citizens that they must only deal with "registered tax accountants." Even people who file their own taxes would have to pay them a small fee to verify who they are. Let private industry take the load off the IRS enforcement division.

And on top of that go back to the old way of paying tax returns with paper checks. They would have to be sent to an actual address instead of some phony electronic account. This would help our bankrupt postal system and insure delivery to real people at real addresses. If the tax return address is phony then the local mailman should notice it. Bingo, you have your criminal.

I am sure the postage would be cheaper than the $5 billion we now give away to identity thieves, many of whom live in other countries. And even if it is not, why reward the identity thieves, many of whom are foreigners? Why should we be subsidizing our enemies when we have enough problems of our own at home?

Enough about taxes. It is time to talk about the largest segment of our society that does not pay any, the Black Subculture (BSC).

See you in Part Two.

PART TWO: UNDERSTANDING THE BLACK SUBCULTURE (BSC)

"It is easier to build strong children than to repair broken men."
—*Fredrick Douglass, the famous African American spokesman.*

AND A LOT cheaper, I might add. We should have taken Fredrick Douglass's advice. Instead we approached our nation's problems with our black brothers and sisters ass backward. Instead of creating strong black families, our federal government for the past 50 years has encouraged and subsidized the creation of dysfunctional black children. Then it spends billions of dollars every year trying to correct the problem once they enter adulthood.

We have to put an end to this insane system and do it quickly. We must attack this problem at its roots instead of depleting our nation's treasury on damage control. It is the only way our bankrupt nation is going to survive. This one simple action would eliminate most of our nation's major social ills in one generation. And it would not cost us the billions we now invest every year in our "War on Poverty." In fact, it would not cost us anything at all so it would save us trillions of dollars in the long run.

First, we have to understand the Black Subculture.

To paraphrase our Pledge of Allegiance, we are TWO nations under God, divided into TWO cultures, not "indivisible" as we say in our Pledge of Allegiance.

The BSC has its own neighborhoods (Watts, Harlem, Hough), its own music (Rap, it used to be Motown), language ("Jive," see the movie *Airplane*), politicians (Congressional Black Caucus), colleges (historically black colleges like Howard University), charities (United Negro College Fund) disease (Sickle Cell Anemia), national holiday (Martin Luther King Day), its own unions (International Association of Black Professional Fire Fighters, the National Black Police Association, etc.), organizations (NAACP), and associations (National Association of Black Journalists etc.) and many more just like them.

As long as African Americans want special treatment it will continue to be difficult for them to join mainstream America.

We have not been one nation under God since the Civil War. And the great question facing our country today is which nation are we going to become when the dust settles in a few decades?

Will we be a free, prosperous, democratic nation like the one our parents left us before the "Great Society?" Or will we become just another Communist dictatorship where our citizens are completely dependent on the government, like it was living in the Soviet Union before we won the Cold War?

As I explained earlier it does not matter if we call it the Black Sub-culture (BSC) or the Black Thug Culture (BTC) that is a sub-culture within the BSC. As long as the BSC has its own agenda which does not blend in with the rest of our country we are on the road to destruction. So let us examine what the BSC is really all about. I firmly believe, dear reader, that once you completely understand the BSC that you will not want to be a part of it. And if you understand the Cleveland councilman's quote that I use to open the next chapter, neither do most black people.

CHAPTER EIGHT:
WHAT EXACTLY IS THE BLACK SUBCULTURE (BSC)?

"I'm sick of living over here, man. I'm just sick of living over here. And I'm a Cleveland councilman. Nobody should have to live through this (expletive) over here. I can't take this (expletive) no more."—Cleveland city councilman Eugene Miller in a recorded conversation with a Cleveland police dispatcher in 2013 when over 100 people were causing a disturbance near his east side home. Reported in the Cleveland Plain Dealer *by Leila Atassi on Sunday April 26. 2015.*

"This is the second time I've called police in two weeks," Bell-Bey said. "My car was surrounded by a bunch of thugs the other night. I've been robbed at gunpoint on East 79th. But this is where we live." —The Cleveland Plain Dealer, *April 19, 2015 in a story by Lynn Ischay titled HONORED ABROAD, ATTACKED AT HOME*

THE SIMPLEST WAY to understand what I mean by the Black Subculture (BSC) is to read the newspaper story that I reference with the second quote above. Once again you can find it on my web site. It pretty much explains the BSC in all its glory.

It is a long story so I will summarize it for you. I could write a dissertation dissecting all the ramifications of this story but I will just hit you with the highlights.

Honey Bell-Bey is a nice black lady who put together a group of inner city black male teens called "The Distinguished Gentlemen of the Spoken Word." They perform poetry, rap and other readings to Cleveland civic groups. It is a valuable program that keeps them off the streets and the *Plain Dealer* gave them a nice bit of publicity when they were raising money to perform in Paris, France.

But they were back on the front page of the Sunday paper when one of the members, twelve-year-old Amir Wilson, was mugged by a gang of about 15 thugs, both boys and girls. Why? So they could steal his cell phone.

"When I was down, about ten girls started stomping me in the face for about two minutes," he said.

So whom did Amir and his friend Josiah Shipp, 14, call after the attack was over? "Amir called his mom. Josiah called Bell-Bey."

So let's stop here for a second and I'll interject with a story from my own life. Why didn't these two youths call their dads? Probably because they don't know where they are. (Reference the "War on Poverty" chapter of this book.)

When I was about Amir's age I was being bullied by a kid in our neighborhood about four years older than me. I don't remember the details but after a while I told my dad about it. My father immediately went down to the neighbor kid's house and had a talk with his father. End of story. Never had a problem with that kid again. In fact, we ended up playing on the same baseball team a few years later.

That doesn't happen in the black community because of the lack of father figures. Instead they use guns or knives to settle arguments. That is another difference between the BSC and the white culture I grew up in. We used our fists to settle arguments when our testosterone levels were acting up. Boxing was an art form that was as natural to us as baseball.

What is great about boxing is that there is a clear winner and loser but after it is over we were taught not to hold a grudge. We'd be right back on the baseball field the next day as if nothing happened.

Now back to Amir's story.

Bell-Bey called the police and they arrived in about 90 seconds and offered to give Amir a ride home. These are the types of police and black youth interactions that do not make the daily news. What if the police saw the mugging, broke it up and one of the thugs got hurt in the process? That would have been in the media for a week and the cops would have been in trouble.

Something is very wrong with our country. Muggings like Amir's happen every day in the BSC but they seldom make the news because they are so common. Only the worst murders, rapes and burglaries are reported and there are plenty of them to fill the paper's crime blotter section every day. Amir was news only because of the previous publicity his group had earned.

How do I know? I worked for 20 years at the fire station near where Amir's incident occurred. We saw this stuff every day. It is only the tip of the iceberg but most Americans are woefully unaware of the BSC lifestyle.

Here's how Amir's mother, Talibah Wilson, explained the BSC's effect on the inner city children: "The streets start to attack them, and they feel they need to have some type of weapon to protect themselves or that they have to join a gang for protection. This is our reality. This is where we live."

And here is the real kicker. Talibah Wilson moved her son Amir to Cleveland from Philadelphia to escape the violence in that city where she saw "drugs go down, people shot, people I know sent to jail."

This shows you how this is not just a Cleveland problem, it is a national one. The BSC is the same ghetto lifestyle in the inner cities of New York City, Chicago, Los Angeles or Houston.

I'll let Honey Bell-Bey summarize the BSC for our readers:

"I live on this street. I would love to say that this is an isolated incident, but these problems in our community are systemic ... This is real. They face this stuff, and worse, every day."

Another story in the *Plain Dealer* gets to the heart of the problem. In the Metro Section's "Newswatch" on May 10, 2015, Mother's Day, there is a story titled: SHOOTING BY ROBBER ANGERS NEIGHBORS.

A gunman shot and killed a 73-year-old woman and a 74-year-old man during a home invasion in one of our BSC neighborhoods.

"The shooting of two people in their 70's angered residents."

"It's absolutely crazy," said Lavelle Shelton, who has lived in the neighborhood for 17 years. "Break-ins are not out of the ordinary but we're not used to this."

"How could you shoot someone in their 70's?" said Robert Ellison, who works in the neighborhood. "These people don't have any morals."

There is the crux of the problem. They don't teach morals in the public schools like they did when we baby boomers were growing up. The teacher would open the school day with a prayer and actually teach the kids about the Ten Commandments even in the public schools. Not anymore.

The liberals argued that it was not proper to teach the Ten Commandments. But they are the basis of our national code of laws and ethics. It is illegal to kill (fifth commandment). It is illegal to steal (seventh commandment). It is illegal to lie (perjury, eighth commandment).

That is why I send my children to parochial schools no matter how good the local schools are. So it is left to the parents to teach their kids morals and the parents in the BSC neighborhoods are dropping the ball.

One more item before I start the second half of my explaining the effect the BSC has on our nation's economy.

There was a story in the May 2015 issue of *Cleveland Magazine* called "It Takes A Village." It was about a group of young black professionals trying to bring back a small part of a desolate BSC neighborhood on Cleveland's east side called Glenville. Good luck to them but here is what the story said they were up against.

"According to Cleveland police figures for 2013 and the first half of

2014, Glenville witnessed 207 aggravated assaults, 423 residential burglaries and 222 drug violations."

And these are only the ones that were reported. There were probably just as many that went unreported. So you can probably double those figures.

It is no coincidence that as America's black population grew so did its prison population. Here is a report from my *The Week Magazine* dated April 24, 2015.

> "The total number of federal, state, county, and local prisoners has ballooned from 320,000 in 1980 to about 2.4 million today—and taxpayers spend more than $80 billion a year to keep all these people locked up. Recidivism rates are appallingly high. About 40 percent of inmates are African-American."

So while I applaud the young urban pioneers, I don't expect them to have much success as long as the BSC is supported by all the government welfare programs.

Let me explain that I am on the same page with these young idealists. I am not throwing my black friends under the bus. What I would like to see happen, and what I firmly believe they would also like to see happen, is for the BSC to become transformed into the BPC, the "Black Prosperous Culture." And if I may be so bold, maybe if they follow some of my advice we could witness that transformation in our lifetimes.

The main thing to understand, my dear reader, is that we will never change the BSC with more government programs. That's what these young people expect, more government programs, more help from foundations and banks. But we've been throwing billions of dollars at the BSC for the past 50 years with no success. Ain't gonna happen.

So I want to start off part two of my book using a story about my father to counter the huge pushback that I will probably receive from black leaders who need the BSC to prosper. (See my chapter on the Black Middle Class.) They are like plantation owners, they have made millions of dollars on the backs of the BSC, and they are not about to see it disappear without a fight.

I can already hear my critics comparing this book to *The Moynihan Report* in 1965.

"You're blaming the victims," they will say.

"I am not blaming anyone but our past Democratic leaders," I will answer them.

"How can you, an old white man, pretend to understand the plight of black people who have been discriminated against all their lives?" they will argue.

Maybe because I was in close contact with the BSC for most of my adult life. And both my father and I were victims of discrimination from black racists. But we never used it as an excuse to become criminals or go on welfare.

First, I will tell you a story about my father, the World War II vet, to illustrate my point. I'll save my own personal story for my chapter on Affirmative Action.

I already told you how my dad fought in World War II, parachuted into France on D-Day and became a prisoner of war because they dropped him in the wrong place. Like many of his generation who grew up in the north, he didn't have a racist bone in his body. I never heard him use the N word or talk badly about Negroes or "colored people." In fact, it was because of white voters like him that Carl Stokes was elected as the first black mayor of a major American city, my home town of Cleveland, Ohio.

Anyway, a few years before qualifying for Social Security he lost his job as an artist. His company was closing up shop and moving to the East Coast. My siblings and I were teenagers and he didn't want to pull us up out of our neighborhood and our schools at such a critical point in our lives. So he applied for a job as a corrections officer in the new county jail and was hired.

I felt bad for him, especially being a prisoner of war himself. I wondered how he would handle his new occupation. Surprisingly, he didn't have many problems with the many black prisoners.

"Every one of them claims that he is innocent," he laughed. He could relate to their concerns. But his fellow black corrections officers treated him like crap. It was his first experience with the BSC and it made him a changed man.

They didn't care about his military background. The sacrifices he made for their country. They didn't care that he helped elect Carl Stokes, the mayor who opened up so many opportunities for their people. The black officers were in the process of taking over the corrections department and all they cared about was that he was a white guy taking a job they wanted to give a black guy. (More on this type of BSC behavior in my chapter on the Black Middle Class.)

The experience changed his perspective on Cleveland's race issues. It was his first experience with the BSC up close and personal. And at about the same time blacks started moving into the public housing project near our family home. Crime was on the upswing in his neighborhood for the first time in my father's lifetime.

My dad's experience is a perfect example of why racism will not go away in contemporary America. The two races will continue to butt heads while trying to live side by side until our federal government stops treating the BSC as our "government approved minority."

Many liberal white people do not understand what I am talking about because they have never had to deal with the BSC. When I spoke to the college students at Oberlin I suggested that instead of joining the Peace Corps and trying to learn about cultures in Asia and Africa they should instead consider spending some time on the east side of Cleveland.

I would like to see all the naïve white college students in America be required before graduation to spend a day just walking around a BSC neighborhood by themselves. Even better, make them spend an evening. Give them a close look at the abandoned houses and gutted-out cars. Call it an urban survival course and give them three credit hours for a day's work.

Or, even better, make them work a part-time job at a convenience store in a BSC neighborhood where they can watch underage kids try to buy a six-pack of beer with food stamps. Anything so that they have to deal with the BSC culture up close and personal like I did. I guarantee we would instantly have a new conversation about race in the United States of America.

Of course, our colleges could never suggest such a thing because their liability costs would go through the roof. Besides, it would turn all those young Democrats into conservative Republicans just like it did me and my dad.

Oh yeah. My dad went way right wing in his old age. He was a changed man from the father I knew growing up. But growing up we didn't have to deal with the BSC. Here's hoping that you do not have to deal with the BSC in your lifetime either. But don't bet on it.

CHAPTER NINE:
WEST TECH AND THE INFAMOUS
SCHOOL BUSING EXPERIMENT

"The aim of West Technical High School is not only to train its students in different school subjects but to aid in the development of each student's personal habits and characteristics so that they will be a help rather than a hindrance when he leaves school...I hope that the school has succeeded in helping each of you to take your place in the social and economic life of our city."
—Principal C.C. Tuck's Farewell Address to the January, 1937 graduating class.

BEFORE WE DISCUSS the infamous "forced school busing experiment" let us make sure we understand one thing. The whole thing was unconstitutional. Don't let anyone tell you otherwise. There was never one local, state or federal legislative body that ever passed a law about forced school busing for racial equality.

Instead a bunch of liberal "activist" federal judges, who believed they knew what was best for us city dwellers, took it upon themselves to force integration in our great cities instead of letting nature take its course. And when they did they ruined the best educational system in the world for millions of American students. And the tragic results are still with us today.

Okay, back to C.C. Tuck. Let's take a moment to reflect on the words of my alma mater's legendary principal, C.C. Tuck, as quoted above. He was known as a tough disciplinarian. But thanks to him that is what West Tech did for about its first sixty years of existence on Cleveland's near west side. It pumped out a huge number of graduates who contributed to our city's and nation's wellbeing. It was not only one of the largest high schools in our nation, it was considered one of the best. It symbolized what free public education in America was all about.

My father went there in the 1940s and I went there in the 1960s and it was still basically the same school. I had the honor of giving the commencement speech when I graduated. So I did some research on its history and discovered that representatives from Germany and Japan visited West Tech after World War II.

(That speech provided the germ for my novel about West Tech in the 1940s: *The West Tech Terrorist, a World War II mystery*.)

Germany and Japan were looking for examples to rebuild their war-torn education systems. They used West Tech as a model to help them grow prosperous economies in their newly democratic countries.

Too bad our black leaders did not have as much sense as our former enemies. In my "There Goes the Neighborhood" chapter I mentioned how the infamous forced school busing experiment chased me out of the city of Cleveland. It also closed West Tech High School. (See my newspaper story on West Tech's last day in the "Voices in the Wilderness" section.)

I promised a more intimate look at school busing, so here it is.

If you want to know what happened to our public school systems thanks to the school busing experiment of the 1980s all you need to do is watch the first ten minutes of a 1989 movie called *Lean on Me*. It takes place in 1987. You don't have to watch the whole movie, just the first ten minutes. The first ten minutes show in graphic detail what happened to the Cleveland schools thanks to school busing. But you should watch the rest of the movie because it is a pretty accurate portrayal of our Black Subculture.

Spoiler alert: Prepare to be shocked. The movie is supposed to be based on a real high school in Paterson, New Jersey, and its tough black principal, Joe Clark, who is played by Morgan Freeman. He arrives on the scene like an old-fashioned cowboy with a bullhorn instead of a six shooter. He saves the dysfunctional school and its students from themselves. East High could be West Tech and Joe Clark could be a black C. C. Tuck.

It opens in 1967 and shows what East High was like when it was mostly white students. That scene reminded me of my days at West Tech since I graduated in 1967. Then it jumps ahead 20 years to show what the school was like after it turned mostly black. It is a bit exaggerated but what really scared me watching it again was how close it came to the West Tech I visited when I returned as a substitute teacher also about 20 years later.

In 1982 I wrote a story about my experiences as a substitute for the Cleveland *Plain Dealer* that I will examine more closely in my "Voices in the Wilderness" section. (It is also reprinted there.) If you read my story and then watch the movie it is amazing how much they have in common. But for now it is important to notice that the movie never once mentions what caused the destruction of both Cleveland's West Tech and Paterson's East High.

FORCED SCHOOL BUSING FOR RACIAL DESEGREGATION.

Need I repeat it again: "Forced School Busing for Racial Desegregation," the culprit that the Democrats never like to discuss.

What the movie does show is how greatly the environment changed in our public schools from the 1960s to the 1980s. There is a scene from the movie when Joe Clark addresses a school assembly and asks all the white kids to stand up. There are only a handful of them. He tells them that they are stuck with him just like the black kids because if they had anywhere else to go they would have left with the rest of them, "them" meaning "white flight."

Sadly, the Cleveland schools did not have any Joe Clarks. Instead, our schools have remained a mess for the past thirty years.

The movie is supposed to be based on a true story. Maybe it did happen once in Paterson, New Jersey. And if it did then Joe Clark should have received the Nobel Peace Prize instead of Barack Obama. Because Joe Clark would have accomplished a miracle yet I am still trying to figure out what Obama did to deserve one.

Back to West Tech. The black Cleveland school principals had a different approach than Joe Clark. If you want to know what happened to Cleveland's public schools when the BSC took over listen to this story from one of West Tech's most respected math teachers. He taught us college prep students pre-calculus in a school that was more geared for teaching vocations like carpentry or auto repair.

Here is what happened the first year after the yellow school buses started shipping students cross town. Mathematics, as you know, builds on what the student has previously learned. You cannot teach a child division until he knows multiplication.

So at the beginning of the school year he gave all his new students a test to gauge their math level comprehension. It was the same test he used in previous years. Except this time all the white students passed the test. And all the black students flunked it.

He knew he had a problem so he took his results to the black principal at his new school. Many of the teachers and administrators were also bused to balance the racial mix. You should hear some of the stories from the white teachers who were bused to the east side along with the students. (SSDAS)

Anyway, my former math teacher told the black principal that the black students would need to take remedial classes. This is what the principal told our awesome math teacher.

"Change the test so all the black kids pass."

Do you believe it? This is all you have to know about how the BSC operates. Didn't he realize that the teacher was talking about mathematics? Something that has been taught in western civilization for about two thousand years.

You can't change the answers in mathematics. Two plus two will always equal four, you can't get around it. It's not discrimination if you don't know the answer. You can't play the race card in math. You either know it or you don't. But he could not care less.

This is a prime example of what the BSC did to the entire Cleveland public school system. It lowered the bar so low that a CPS diploma became meaningless.

The math teacher's story made complete sense to me the moment I heard it because I had many similar experiences during my career as a substitute teacher in the Cleveland school system. (That experience was one of the main reasons that I changed my political views from a liberal Democrat to a conservative Republican.)

Let me tell you a couple more quick stories before we go into the details of the school busing fiasco. I could tell you tons of them but maybe this one will seal the deal.

As a substitute teacher I taught in most of the junior high and high schools in Cleveland. They would call me in the morning, give me an assignment and I would go. I taught everything from machine shop to American history.

On one of my first days in the Cleveland schools, I walked in the front door of a west side junior high school that was new to me. The first thing I saw was a black girl putting a big knife in her locker. Since I knew such a thing would never be allowed at Dear Old West Tech (our alma mater song), I took her and her knife with me to the front office.

On the way there she said to me: "You don't like black people, do you?"

I would soon learn that blaming whitey is another pillar of the BSC. If in trouble always play the race card. It is always whitey's fault for all your difficulties in life.

When we got to the front office I turned her over to an assistant principal. At West Tech they would have called her parents to come get her and she would have received an instant suspension. But at West Tech no one would have dared to bring a knife or gun into the school in the first place.

I quickly learned that in the new BSC-controlled Cleveland public school system there was a different attitude in play. The black female assistant principal looked at me like I was crazy. What did I expect her to do with the student? She took the knife and just sent her on her way.

I later learned the reason why they did not discipline students in the new Cleveland schools like they did at Dear Old West Tech. If they did they would have to fill out a form and send it downtown. And the media was watching the statistics to see how the busing experiment was going.

If there were too many suspensions it made them look bad, as if they couldn't handle the students, which they couldn't. So the inmates were left free to run the asylums. And the media thought everything was wonderful. Meanwhile those of us on the inside experienced a completely different environment than what the media was selling the public.

Don't believe me? Here's one more quick story to illustrate my point. I was driving downtown on a day off and I was stuck in a traffic jam on the interstate highway right below a pedestrian bridge. I looked up and saw a junior high student throwing rocks through the fence at the cars below.

Fortunately our cars were not moving. I do not know if you can comprehend, dear reader, what a rock can do when it hits the windshield of a car moving 60 miles per hour. It is not a pretty sight. I eyeballed the kid and I knew which Cleveland junior high was at the other end of the pedestrian bridge. So I stopped by the school on my way downtown.

Once again I found a black female assistant principal and told her my story. I even gave her the description of the kid but she was not interested. She did not know who it was and did not care to find out.

So I left. But on my way out the door, lo and behold, there is the stone-throwing culprit being punished by standing outside the door of his classroom. He must have been a big troublemaker. So I go back to the principal's office and tell her the perpetrator is standing right outside door number such and such. Once again she could not care less.

Two weeks later someone threw a rock from a different interstate highway and caused life-threatening injuries to the two front seat passengers of a speeding car. Was it the same kid? Probably not. But if some parent went out of his way to finger a West Tech student behaving dangerously when I was in school the punishment would have been swift and hurtful.

News flash. Just as this book is going to press an Amtrak train crashed as it sped "through one of the poorest and most violent parts of Philadelphia" (code for BSC). The accident killed eight people and injured over 200. And there is speculation that the engineer may have been struck by a rock or a bullet through the front windshield.

This in turn reminded me of another story. I took an Amtrak from Cleveland to San Francisco on my honeymoon. When we went through the black section of Oakland someone shot a bullet through the train's window.

Welcome to the new world of the BSC. It would take a couple decades before the public and the media finally acknowledged that the school busing experiment was a total disaster for both the city of Cleveland and the Cleveland public school system.

Even George Forbes, the former Cleveland City Council president and former president of the Cleveland chapter of the NAACP, eventually admitted that school busing was a terrible mistake. It was a huge mistake not only in Cleveland but on the national level as well.

That is why you seldom hear the Democrats or the media discuss the great "school busing experiment" of the 1980s. Mainly because, thanks to their misguided ideas, school busing destroyed all our great cities and their wonderful public school systems.

Don't believe me? In 2012 the schools unveiled one of their many new plans to fix the school system. They come up with one every five years or so. This one was called the "Cleveland Plan for Transforming Schools." Here's what the plan admitted in 2012: "Currently 55 percent of Cleveland schools are failing to meet even minimum state standards."

No kidding? So in 2015 they bragged that they raised the graduation rate 12 percent, all the way up to 64 percent and declared their latest plan a success. If you read between the lines it means that a few years back, after a series of different reform plans, graduation rate was still only 52 percent. And to be honest a lot of those kids probably shouldn't even be given a high school diploma. They were merely pushed up the ladder to move them out of the system and pump up the rates.

Great job, eh? When I was at West Tech the graduation rate and attendance rate were both near 100 percent. Thank you, Democrats. I also took two buses to get to West Tech but not the free yellow school buses. I had to pay to ride the Cleveland Transit System buses with the rest of the general population. Even that little cost was a strain on my family's tight budget. But believe me, that was a learning experience well worth the coins.

Forced cross-town school busing was another cause championed by the Democratic Party. It was the brainchild of Democratic President John F. Kennedy's think tank, "the best and the brightest," the same guys who gave us the Vietnam War.

I wonder if they even teach our children about the "school busing experiment" in today's history books? Probably not. And if they do, I'm sure they give it a different slant than mine.

I know that sociologists, most of whom grew up in the suburbs and never set foot in an inner city neighborhood in their entire lives, like to blame "white flight" for the destruction of our big city's schools and neighborhoods. They don't like to reference the school busing experiment that caused the "white flight" in the first place.

As if they wouldn't mind sending their own children on an hour-long bus ride to a neighborhood and school controlled by the BTC. They might as well have put our kids on a bus to Baghdad. No one ever investigates the damage it did to white children in the name of helping black children. (SSDAS)

The school busing experiment was so wrong in so many ways it is almost impossible to list them all. For one thing it destroyed the wonderful after-school activities that were available to my generation. At West Tech we had everything from Thespians to Future Teachers of America to a Ski Club to a full-fledged Orchestra, Choir and Marching Band. You can't stay after school to play your violin or act in the school play if you have to catch the cross-town school bus home. What a tragedy. They ripped the guts out of everything that made high school fun.

It also bankrupted our nation's big city school systems. The Federal Judges who ordered the busing left it to the school boards to figure out how to pay for it. How was the school board supposed to magically find the funds to pay for the costs of all the new buses? Not to mention the salaries for the new useless administrators, the shady lawyer fees and the increased cost for security once the BSC flourished.

When I was at West Tech our only security was a 98-pound woman sitting at a desk by the school's entrance. She was called a hall monitor. But she ruled 3500 students with an iron hand. If she put the finger on you, you were toast, baby.

After the school busing experiment spread the BSC throughout the entire school system, it had to pay millions of dollars for metal detectors at all the entrances and armed Cleveland cops to roam the hallways. Imagine going to a school like that? Even the head of the NAACP admitted that today's Cleveland schools resemble prisons more than institutions of education. But that is a necessity of living in the BSC.

There are so many different ramifications to the whole affair that I could write a book on it. But that would be an uphill battle in our current politically correct climate. I'll leave that idea for someone else.

There is one last subject that comes out of trying to teach in the BSC neighborhoods that I would like to address. I call it "teacher abuse" and it is another subject that the media never covers.

First let me say, that I must have been a pretty good sub since they called me every morning with a different assignment. Or maybe they just could not find enough teachers crazy enough to enter the Cleveland schools. As long as no student got hurt and there was no damage to the classroom it was considered a successful school day. That is just how far school busing lowered the bar in the Cleveland public school system.

I was basically a babysitter as a sub in the Cleveland city schools. There were seldom lesson plans available and most of the kids would cut class anyway because there was no one to stop them. There was no punishment for it. So I just bided the hours and watched the clock. To pass the time I would engage the students in conversation. Pick their minds, so to speak.

One of my first questions would be: "Where's your regular teacher?" You don't know how many times I was told they were off for a month or two because of injuries from dealing with the BTC environment. A typical response would be: "Oh, he broke his arm trying to break up a fight in the hallways." Then they would laugh. They thought it was funny that their teacher would even attempt such a thing.

Teacher abuse is the dirty little secret of the Cleveland public school system and most other big city school districts. The media does not touch it. But it is a damn shame what teachers have to put up with in the BSC schools. It is similar to what Cleveland cops must contend with on the streets of the BSC neighborhoods. It is also the reason so many teachers leave the profession early. (SSDAS)

I have one last sub story that is perfectly suited to illustrate the plague of teacher abuse infecting the Cleveland schools since the arrival of the BSC. It is from the time that I was assigned to teach in my old homeroom at my old West Tech high school. It should have been an exciting day filled with pleasant nostalgia. It turned out to be just the opposite. Instead it clearly shows how the breakdown in discipline within the Cleveland schools makes it impossible for teachers to teach and students to learn.

My homeroom was a shop class in the basement. (Don't get me going about the loss of shop classes in today's schools, that's another subject that deserves a national debate.) About five minutes into the class one of the students decided to leave.

I foolishly tried to stop him. Instead of sitting back down and listening to his teacher as we would have done, he went berserk on me. He grabbed an iron bar from a tool box and started chasing me around the room. I had to dance around the classroom and use the shop class tables to keep him away from me while I tried to calm him down.

So what did his fellow students do? Were they shocked that a student would act like that toward a teacher? Did they come to my rescue? Go ask for help at the principal's office? Hell no, instead they cheered him on. This is the BTC at its finest.

Think I'm making this up? No way Jose. I wrote a story about my substituting experiences for the Cleveland *Plain Dealer Sunday Magazine* and I opened it with this experience. You can find the entire story at the end of this book.

You need to read the *Plain Dealer* story for the details but only the appearance of a uniformed security guard saved my butt. There is a similar scene in the opening ten minutes of the *Lean on Me* movie. A white teacher tries to break up a fight and gets his head bashed. The firemen take him away in an ambulance. I saw my share of similar occurrences from my fireman's job as well as my substituting position.

Sadly, this is typical of the atmosphere the Cleveland public school teacher is expected to teach in. Anyone who teaches in a big city urban school district should get combat pay like they do in the army. Later when I shared my experience with other teachers in the teacher's lounge, each one could spin a similar horror story.

But do you want to know what the worst thing about the entire experience was? His punishment.

After class I followed up with the administration about his discipline. I was told that he was a chronic troublemaker and they suspended him. But the very next day I saw him roaming the hallways of West Tech. I saw him in a pack of students and he just smiled at me before disappearing into the crowd. What happened?

Easy. Even though he was suspended he still took the bus from the east side to West Tech and basically had a couple free days to roam around the school or the surrounding neighborhood and cause more trouble. Who would invent such a system? Thank you, BSC, for taking care of business.

Once again, *Lean on Me* had a similar scene. Principal Joe Clark expels all the thugs so the teachers can get on with the teaching but then one of the thugs comes back into the building and picks a fight with another student. Then he pulls a knife on Principal Clark when he tries to break it up. I'll let you watch the movie to see how that turns out. But talk about art imitating life.

If the Cleveland public schools really wanted to educate their children and bring up their test scores they would do just what Joe Clark did, throw about half the students out of the schools once and for all. Force the parents of disruptive kids to educate them with home schooling. They are just taking up space and making it impossible to educate the students who actually do want to learn something.

Only let students remain who understand that an education is a privilege not a right. Of course, you know, that is not going to happen. Instead they expect the poor teachers to perform miracles and turn their juvenile delinquents into Rhodes Scholars without any backup from their parents or the school administration.

How did we come to such a sorry state of affairs? You can thank the NAACP and the Democrats for inventing the BSC and all of its ramifications.

Education starts at home, everyone knows that. But many of our black citizens and their leaders won't acknowledge it. They expect the government to do everything for them. They want free kindergarten and free pre-school and free child care while adding nothing to our city's or nation's coffers.

Many of our liberal academics and sociologists think that's a great idea. More free child care will solve all our problems. But that's Communism, people. Basically, they just want someone to watch their kids at an earlier and earlier age so they can make more babies and receive more free stuff from the government.

When I was growing up it was our parents' job to prepare us for kindergarten. We were expected to know our letters and numbers when we walked in the door on the first day of school.

In fact, the real irony here is that the one of the great fears of Americans in the 1950s was that the government would take away our children and brainwash them like the Russian Communists and German Nazis did under Stalin and Hitler. Yet today's moms voluntarily drop their children off at day care centers at an earlier and earlier age.

Here is one last insight that I would like to share with you about unwed teenage moms. It shows the total breakdown of our social mores from my baby boomer generation to the present one.

When I graduated from West Tech we did have a classmate who was pregnant. Everyone knew who she was and I am sure she was completely embarrassed about it. But looking back it was not too surprising since our graduating class numbered over 500 students in a student body of 3500 students. (If those numbers do not make sense it is because we had so many students that we had both January and June graduations.) Interestingly, Paterson, New Jersey's East High had about the same number of students.

Anyway, the important thing is that soon after graduation the guy who knocked her up married her. Fast forward twenty years later when the school busing experiment was in full swing. When I was subbing at Dear Old West Tech they actually had a day care center in the school where all the unwed moms could drop off their babies while attending class. Free child care, yippee!

Yet their parents often complained that there was not enough money being spent on our inner city schools. Surprisingly, Cleveland's per student expenditure was one of the highest in the state, thanks to all the freebies. But with terrible results. Once again, thank you, BSC, for producing children who are a drain on our treasury from their cradles to their graves.

On that note let me suggest that you listen to a song from my school days. It was a popular song from Motown, the black record label from Detroit that both black and white kids enjoyed. It was called "Love Child" by Diana Ross and the Supremes, a black female group.

The song is about an unmarried woman who asks her boyfriend not to pressure her into sleeping with him for fear of creating a "love child," a baby without a father. Especially since she was a "love child" herself who had grown up poor and without a father. Can you believe that it was a number one hit song in 1968?

Imagine trying to release a rap song like that in the black community today? You would be laughed out of existence. And you wonder why our inner cities are dying a slow painful death?

Here's something that we need to look at. It has been my observation that the larger the role of the BSC in a school system the lower its test scores and the lower its total rankings against other schools. Someone should do a study. (SSDAS) The best schools in America are those that are the furthest away from our inner cities. What should we do?

I promised in the last chapter to give you, my curious readers, my solution to the Cleveland school disaster. Is there any way to restore them to their former glory? Yes there is.

But before we address the Cleveland schools' problem, let's try this for all of our nation's school problems. What is the most important aspect of our schools? The teachers, of course. And whom do we neglect the most? Why the teachers, of course.

The Federal judges who started school busing never asked the teachers what they thought of the idea. Kind of like the same guys who invented Obamacare never asked the doctors for their opinion. They just rammed it down our throats.

I propose we start a Federal minimum wage for teachers at let's say $100,000 a year. Forget raising the minimum wage for fast food workers. That is supposed to an entry level position. You aren't supposed to raise a family working at McDonalds. (I once worked at McDonalds but that is another story.)

I am surprised that we can even find any teachers to fill the positions thanks to all they have to put up with in our modern schools. That is why so many college education majors give up on the profession. If we guarantee them $100,000 a year, suddenly we will have our best and brightest fighting for the spots. Besides, we need to help them pay off their student loans.

We trust our teachers with our most important resource, our children and our future leaders. We should make sure that they represent the finest men and women America has to offer. Our schools would once again become the best on the planet.

If the Cleveland schools just took the money they spend on metal detectors and armed guards they would be able to give all their teachers a big raise.

Now here is my plan for saving the Cleveland public school system. I offered up my ideas in an opinion piece published in the *Plain Dealer* back in 1996, almost twenty years ago. It was Cleveland's bicentennial birthday and I thought we needed drastic solutions to our city's most nagging problems.

(This story is also reprinted at the end of this book.)

What I proposed is very simple and is based on a very simple obser-vation. The Cleveland schools suck because they are too big and too corrupt. Too many people are sucking money from them. That is why no one wants to change the system. Meanwhile the schools in the suburbs are still doing well as long as the federal government stays out of them. (Beware of Common Core.)

So what I proposed was eliminating the city of Cleveland. It was 200 years old and beginning to show its age. It would be broken into six suburbs based on the fact that it had six police districts and six fire battalions. But the key was that once you eliminated the city of Cleveland you also eliminated the Cleveland school system, breaking it into six much smaller, more manageable units.

Since I published that piece a lot has happened to our city. First, the media finally discovered the corruption that pervaded our county gov-ernment and sent a bunch of county officials to jail. Cuyahoga county, like the city of Cleveland, was controlled by one party, the Democrats, and ripe for corruption. After the smoke cleared we changed our county government but the new plan fell far short of what I proposed because it left the city of Cleveland intact, the great big elephant sitting in the room.

Second, downtown Cleveland started booming. After decades of neglect it finally turned into an entertainment and housing neighbor-hood, much like our country's other great cities. Cities like New York, Chicago and San Francisco come to mind. Our success is finally being noticed by the rest of the country. The result was landing the prestigious Republican National Convention for the summer of 2016.

So the local board of commerce is now marketing Cleveland as "CLE" which is all well and good. The problem is that our city's neighborhoods are still controlled by the BSC. So what we have here is the same dilemma facing most of our country's great cities. The CLE is clashing with the BSC. Who is going to win?

If the BSC wins we are doomed as a city AND a nation. Blacks and whites alike are always writing letters to the *Plain Dealer* complaining that the city government spends too much money on downtown as opposed to the neighborhoods. But throwing money at the problem is the federal government's solution to everything and it hasn't worked in 50 years, in fact it made everything worse.

So I am proposing that we eliminate the BSC just like we need to eliminate the city of Cleveland. Of course, since Cleveland is now a primarily black city, I expect to be labelled a "racist" for suggesting such a thing. That is another hollow argument often used by black leaders who feed off the BSC. They need the BSC to support their cozy lifestyle. (We will explore this phenomenon later when we discuss the black middle class.)

If my fellow black citizens would step back and inspect my arguments maybe they would realize that my solution would make their lives much better also. So here and now I am going to show you some of the effects the BSC has had on the great city that I grew up in. If the BSC is allowed to continue to grow and multiply then there will be more of these disasters in the future. Or we can get smart, tell the federal government to quit subsidizing the BSC and leave us alone so we can prosper, both blacks and whites living in harmony.

CHAPTER TEN:
THE BSC AND THE CLE

"At least six white adults were attacked near Public Square without provocation by roaming bands of young African-Americans described as juveniles. One of the victims, a 23 year old man from Akron, woke up in an ambulance after being ambushed."—African American Plain Dealer *columnist Phillip Morris in a column on April 8, 2015.*

THE "CLE" IS the new brand for Cleveland compliments of its chamber of commerce, The Greater Cleveland Partnership. And Cleveland IS making another comeback. Witness our winning the competition as host of the Republican National Convention in 2016. Downtown is booming even if our neighborhoods are hemorrhaging citizens.

So the story above about six adults from the suburbs being mugged during Cleveland's annual St. Patrick's Day parade on March 17, 2015, was barely reported in the local news media. However, a courageous black newspaper columnist and an outspoken black Cleveland city councilman eventually turned the spotlight on the race angle. In typical fashion, the white media could not dare mention the races of the attackers and their victims without being labeled "racist."

As a Cleveland fireman I saw many similar scenarios during my long career in our fair city. But they were seldom reported by the media for the reason stated above. Based on my experiences, as soon as I read the story I figured it was black youths beating up white partiers. It was only because it happened on St. Patrick's Day, when thousands of white suburbanites spend money in downtown Cleveland, that Cleveland councilman Zack Reed spoke up and called it what it was.

Here's African American columnist Phillip Morris reporting on African American Cleveland councilman, Zack Reed.

"He (Zack Reed) is calling them hate crimes ... Public Square "is ground zero for blacks to go beat up whites," Reed said in an interview with the Northeast Ohio Media Group. "I believe this is a hate crime because it is black folks purposely going downtown to beat up white folks."

Here is how Morris explained the phenomenon:

"It's called the 'knockout game.' Young violent thugs play it on occasion."

And here's the kicker. Morris asked what if a band of white kids attacked some black partiers at the annual African American Luke Easter Park "Family Unity Event in the Park"? Here's the reaction he would expect:

"The event would make national news and every civil rights leader worth his pepper would parachute into Cleveland with megaphones blaring. The town would erupt in flames and instantly become the epicenter of America's hysterical reporting on racial conflicts and hostilities."

Amen to that, my brother.

This is the phenomenon that I want to explore in this chapter. How the violent Black Subculture changed the entire fabric of the city of Cleveland where I grew up.

What happened on St. Patrick's Day, 2015, in downtown Cleveland has happened again and again across our city's historical landscape and our once great metropolis has suffered much in the aftermath. But these causes and results are seldom mentioned in our media, once again for the reason stated above.

In the previous chapter I showed how the BSC destroyed our once great Cleveland public school system. In this chapter I am going to list a whole litany of cultural events that were likewise eliminated. What is important to understand is that when we lost each of the assets below it hurt our local economy as much as our civic pride.

I am not going to go into a lot of details with each event because that would take too long and be too repetitious. However, I want to start off with one personal story to make my point. Then I will show how the other events are similar in nature.

This is one of my stories from my career as a Yellow Cab driver. Back in the 1990s the city of Cleveland was making an exciting comeback from its earlier reputation as "The Mistake on the Lake."

And one of its most visible and celebrated accomplishments was the huge entertainment complex that sprang up along the banks of the Cuyahoga River, the same river that gained international notoriety in the 1960s for catching on fire (which was one of the main reasons for our earlier bad reputation). The dance clubs, bars and restaurants that lined the river were called "The Flats." And its reputation was also growing by leaps and bounds.

So when I picked up four Japanese businessmen at the airport in my cab the first thing they asked me was if I knew where The Flats were. Of course I did. I told them that it was their lucky day because there was a big celebration going on called "Riverfest."

If you want to capture the flavor of "Riverfest" reference the photo on the cover of my book, CLEVELAND: *Where the East Coast Meets the Midwest*. It shows huge throngs of partiers and boats crowding the river banks at a previous "Riverfest." The Flats had become a destination for young adults from all over Ohio and even eastern Pennsylvania, western Indiana and northern Kentucky.

So the Japanese businessmen asked me to wait while they went to their hotel and changed. If I took them to The Flats they would give me a nice tip. So I did.

I dropped them off in front of one of the booming dance clubs and wished them luck. It was one of the most regretful actions of my cab driving career. Why?

Because there was a riot going on in The Flats and I was unaware of it. Just after I dropped them off I saw a Cleveland fire department rescue squad pulling up to a bar and since I was a Cleveland fire fighter at the time I asked them what was going on.

They told me someone had been shot. They explained to me that the black kids from the projects that were located along the rim of the land above The Flats were "wilding." It was just like the "knockout game" the thugs were playing this past St. Patrick's Day but on a much larger scale. Gangs of young blacks were mugging the naïve white suburbanites coming out of the bars and clubs a bit tipsy.

I felt very sorry for dropping those Japanese tourists in the middle of it. I spent the rest of the evening giving free rides to desperate white kids trying to get back to their cars safely. I remember one crying pregnant girl who had lost her friends and was rightfully afraid for her unborn baby. I gave her a free ride back to her west side residence.

Of course, the local media downplayed the riot. It was barely mentioned in the papers for two reasons. First, they didn't want to kill the golden lamb. The Flats were bringing large amounts of tax revenues and jobs into the city of Cleveland and bad publicity would hurt the income flow. And of course they couldn't mention the racial angle. That was a big no-no just like it is today.

Actually, this was nothing new. The muggings were happening before "Riverfest" and would continue to happen for a few years after. As a Cleveland fireman we often responded to these incidents. They usually happened when the bars were closing and the young adults were stagger-ing back to their cars. Easy pickings for the black thugs.

Even though the media overlooked the problem they could not save The Flats. Word of mouth is a powerful force. It wasn't long after the Riverfest Riot that bars and clubs started closing. Within a few years there were only a handful of businesses left. The once great Flats became a ghost town of boarded-up bars. All that tax income and job opportunities, for both blacks and whites, disappeared. Thank you, BSC.

What is really interesting is whenever the death of The Flats comes up in newspaper columns or on radio talk shows they blame it on unruly kids over-partying. They never mention the racial crime factor.

One more quick story before I list my top seven victims of the BSC. When I graduated from high school in 1967 I won a prestigious journalism scholarship called the Ed Bang Scholarship. It was named after a legend-ary local sports writer whose friends started it to honor him. Only two high school seniors in all of Cuyahoga County won it each year.

So I was invited to a big dinner in a downtown hotel to receive my award. All of Cleveland's movers and shakers were there. I sat at a table with a bunch of them. And all they talked about all evening was how the recent election of African American mayor Carl Stokes and the "colored people" were ruining the city.

Of course, since I was a naïve high school senior, I thought they were a bunch of racists. I took pride on my dad voting for Mayor Carl Stokes and I would have voted for him myself if I was old enough. But looking back at that event from today's perspective it turns out they were correct.

Our fair city was changing dramatically but I was not aware enough to notice it. Here are a few examples of the many Cleveland traditions that disappeared from my youth after the BSC invaded our community. Will our annual St. Patrick's Day parade be next?

Number one: The annual Thanksgiving Day Charity Football game.

High school football was huge in Cleveland throughout the 1940s, 50s and 60s. There were two leagues, the West Senate from schools on the west side of the Cuyahoga River and the East Senate on the east side. Up to 70,000 fans would fill Cleveland Stadium every Thanksgiving Day to watch the City High School Championship Game between the two league champs. That is unheard of for a high school football game. The ticket money went to a charity sponsored by our local newspaper, the Cleveland *Plain Dealer*. Thus, the Charity Game moniker.

It was a great tradition until our black high school population grew on the east side. And as it grew so did the number of fights after the game. The last Charity game was played in 1968. The concept was brought back in 2005 but it was only a shadow of its former self. The irony is that a lot of the money raised was used to help poor black families. Chalk another one up for the BSC.

Number two: Friday night lights.

When I was in school not only did we have the annual charity game but every Friday night in the fall we had high school football games. At West Tech we had the premier field on the west side and hosted not only our home games but also games from other schools. It was not unusual for over 10,000 high school fans, parents and alumni to attend the game with a rousing half-time show by the school marching band.

Today you can watch a Cleveland public school football game on one of the city's public cable channels. We would watch them at the fire station.

They are now played on Saturday afternoons in front of mostly empty stands. I wonder why? Think the BTC's tactics after the night games had anything to do with it?

The suburbs still have Friday night football games. One more reason to break the city into six suburbs.

Number three: Our lakefront parks.

Cleveland was blessed with a couple of large lakefront parks on Lake Erie that offered a nice respite from the summer heat. Thousands of swimmers would crowd the beaches every summer. Once again that all changed as the Black Subculture grew along with safety concerns. The beaches are still there but they remain practically empty even on our hottest summer days.

Number four: Fourth of July Fireworks.

When I was a kid we would go to Edgewater Park along Lake Erie (see above) with 100,000 other residents to celebrate our great country's founding with picnics and fireworks. Once again, as the BSC grew so did the fights and crimes. So for a while the fireworks also disappeared. Today they have been resurrected with a mini-celebration on our downtown's Public Square but the crowds are quite thin compared to the good old days at Edgewater Park.

Number five: Euclid Beach Park.

This was an amusement park also along our lakefront. It was like having Disney World just a bus ride away. It was so popular that President Kennedy attracted over 100,000 visitors when he gave a campaign speech there in 1960. But it had the misfortune of being located on the city's east side, near where the BSC was growing. It closed in 1969.

Number Six: Geauga Lake Park.

A similar fate fell to another amusement park in the eastern suburbs. It was called Geauga Lake Park. It was a larger version of Euclid Beach Park and it lasted longer because it was further away from Cleveland's inner city problems.

In 2004 new owners pumped $140 million in capital improvements into the park but attendance fell drastically anyway and the park closed in 2007. Why?

Well, the last time I visited the park with my young children I experienced two racial incidents. They reminded me of my experience on my grandmother's street. So I never went back and I guess a lot of other white visitors shared the same experience.

And who were hurt the most by the park's closing? All the minority workers who lost their jobs, that's who.

Number seven: Indoor malls.

Randall Park Mall on the city's east side once billed itself as the largest indoor mall in the country. Indoor malls mushroomed all over Cleveland's suburbs in the 1950s and 1960s. They were a great innovative idea. Who doesn't want to shop indoors during Northeast Ohio's brutal winters? But the planners did not factor in the BSC.

I remember doing a book signing at Randall Park mall. They put me behind a table in front of the book store so I could attract shoppers who were just walking by, customers who weren't even planning to stop in the book store. While sitting there I would watch groups of black juveniles roaming the mall.

The center of the mall was filled with kiosks and the black kids would have one of their gang distract the employee while the other ones would shoplift some items. It happened so often I figured the vendors just chalked it up to the cost of doing business. I figured they followed a similar pattern inside the stores and food courts.

Then I saw the same modus operandi at other east side malls like

Euclid Square Mall. Both of those malls have since been torn down. Was the BTC factor at work? That would be my guess.

I could go on and on but no use going into overkill. I think you get the idea. The same black thugs who are screaming police brutality and sparking demonstrations of support across our nation in 2015 did serious damage to the city of Cleveland's social and economic fabric during my lifetime.

It is time we took a look at how the Cleveland Police Department (CPD) and the BSC deal with each other on a daily basis. It is no fun being a Cleveland cop on the mean streets of Cleveland's inner city neighborhoods.

Next chapter please.

CHAPTER ELEVEN:
THE BSC AND THE CPD

"Each successive generation of young punks makes it more difficult to break concentric circles of dysfunction, hopelessness, despair and violence. ... Damn punks are the core of the problem—not blue uniforms."
—Phillip Morris, an African-American Plain Dealer *columnist, commenting on two police officers wounded in Ferguson, Missouri, on March 12, 2015.*

I STARTED WRITING this book in the year 2014. That was the year that white cops killing blacks was making national headlines. First, there was the Ferguson, Missouri cop who shot a white teenager and sparked protests all around the country. Then there was the white New York City cop who allegedly killed a black homeless guy with a choke hold. It also sparked national protests.

I won't go into those incidents very much because right here in my hometown of Cleveland, Ohio we had a couple of our own cases that also fed the national media frenzy. One concerns a deadly police chase in 2012 and the other is the killing of an unarmed black youth by a rookie white cop. Since they are local and I am more familiar with these cases I will use them to help me illustrate the problems at the root of the BSC.

If you look at them closely they will reveal how difficult it is for both white and black cops to work in a BSC neighborhood. I want to discuss some aspects of these events that the national media overlooks. It will help you understand where my views come from.

The first thing you have to understand is that the Cleveland Police Department (CPD) arrested over 31,000 people in 2014. That's a lot of criminals roaming our streets. That doesn't even count all the criminals who got away without being arrested.

Considering all the rampant crime in our BSC neighborhoods you would expect its citizens to be praising our police officers for their sacrifices instead of criticizing them for a few rare incidents. Instead they want to blame the police for all their problems.

One of their biggest criticisms is that the CPD is biased against black people. But if a cop works in Cleveland's Fourth District and 98 percent of its residents are black there is a pretty good chance most of the cop's arrests are going to be African Americans. If the U.S. Justice Department has its way the Fourth District cops are going to have to start arresting any white suburbanite who passes through on his way to work downtown just to balance the statistics.

Thank God the feds came to our town to show us the light.

I've been saying all along that the problem with our inner cities is not the cops, it is the neighborhoods they have to work in. So far we have covered Section 8 housing and the School Busing experiment as two of the ways that the BSC destroyed Cleveland's once prosperous and proud neighborhoods. A third major component of the BSC influence is the spike in criminal activities tied to its arrival.

But I realize that you are not going to take my word for it. I need some specific examples to prove to my curious readers that I know what I am talking about. So I asked myself: what should I do?

I decided maybe we should examine the two stories from the CPD's files that I mentioned earlier. They both attracted national media interest. First there was the deadly police chase that resulted in the death of two "unarmed black adults." Then there was the police shooting of a black youth, Tamir Rice, brandishing a toy gun.

But there was also a third case that the media seemed to forget so you probably did not hear about. A Cleveland cop killed another unarmed black youth, Brandon Jones, while he was allegedly robbing a neighborhood convenience store even more recently, March 19, 2015. On the radio I heard the store's owner, an elderly black guy who lived there for years, thank the cops for doing their duty. That story died so fast it made my head spin.

I wondered why. Then I heard a local television station report that both officers involved in the shooting were African American cops. That's why you don't hear anything about it. No media frenzy or violent protests about that shooting. Three months later the police chase and Tamir Rice are still in the papers almost every day yet I am still waiting for the media to cover the convenience store story.

How do you think the white cops on the CPD feel about their black chief and black mayor after that scenario? Local black leaders are still organizing protests about Tamir Rice but I hear nothing mentioned about Brandon Jones. Sounds like racial discrimination to me.

Maybe it has something to do with what *Plain Dealer* columnist Mark Naymik added to a column about the U.S. Department of Justice's settlement with the Cleveland Police Department.

On May 27, 2015 he commented:

"Recruiting black officers is one of the ultimate goals of the reforms. The city and Justice Department believe hiring more black officers from urban areas will go a long way toward building trust among Cleveland residents."

That is the real reason behind this national persecution of white cops doing their job in black neighborhoods. Black leaders want more government jobs for their constituents. I'll go in more detail as to how that idea played out in my chapter on Affirmative Action.

For now, let's go back to the two Cleveland police incidents that are driving the media coverage. Both incidents have been portrayed in the media and by black leaders as examples of police brutality that exposed our society's inherent racism. Each one sparked protests and outrage by everyone from Barak Obama to his good friend Al Sharpton. I think that maybe we need to take a closer look at both of these incidents in light of my challenge to these assumptions.

I did mention in a previous chapter that almost every day there are stories about the BSC in my morning newspaper, the Cleveland *Plain Dealer*. Blacks kill and rob other blacks with guns at an amazing pace.

However, these stories are never framed within the context of the BSC. That is because neither the reporters nor you, the reader, know how to connect the dots. That is one of the main objects of this book, to teach you how to connect the dots.

So today, November 19, 2014, as I am writing this book, I open up my *Plain Dealer* hoping to find a couple of examples of the BSC to support my argument. And lo and behold I hit the jackpot. There are a number of stories so obviously related to the BTC that no explanation is necessary.

It is like I won the Ohio Lottery. Or even better, it is like winning a Section 8 housing subsidy from CMHA.

There is a front-page story under the subject head: "Deadly Police Chase." The headline is: "Judge Approves $3 Million Settlement." The sub-headline is: "Russell, Williams Families Each Get About $865,000 After Lawyer Fees."

This the perfect example of the BSC in action and how it costs tax-payers millions of dollars. But before we go any further please remember as you read this that the three-million-dollar settlement comes out of the city of Cleveland's general fund. This is the money that the city government needs to operate on a daily basis. Do you know how many cops we could hire with that money? Or fire trucks we could buy? I wonder how many hard-working Cleveland citizens have to pay their yearly taxes to generate $3 million? (SSDAS)

First, we will look at reporter John Caniglia's story about the deadly police chase. It gives an overview of the whole case and the $3 million settlement. But more importantly he also wrote a side story about the families that received the settlement. That's where the real action is. I will quote him often. Here goes, hold on for the ride of your life.

Back on November 29, 2012 Cleveland police tried to pull over a car driven by Timothy Russell for speeding. His passenger was Malissa Williams. But Timothy did not want to stop so he took off. Why? Who knows, maybe he was out looking for drugs, maybe he even had some in his possession, maybe he thought they were looking for him as part of another criminal investigation. He had a rap sheet as long as my arm. And it was later reported that both of them had cocaine in their blood systems.

The policemen trying to stop them thought Timothy fired shots at them and said so to their radio dispatcher. That info was relayed to other police officers throughout the city. (Their family's defense lawyers would later claim that they were unarmed and that the noise the cops heard was their old car backfiring. Maybe so or maybe they did have a gun and threw it away during the chase. Who knows?) So the Cleveland Police Department did what any organization does when it is attacked. Its members came to the defense of their comrades.

Russell led the cops on a long and dangerous chase. He reached speeds of over 100 MPH driving through many of the city's predominantly black neighborhoods, making it to the suburbs before he was finally surrounded in an East Cleveland middle school parking lot. (There will be a chapter on the suburb of East Cleveland later.)

But he still did not stop. He kept driving toward the officers. So they opened fire and pumped over 100 shots into his car, killing both the driver Russell and his passenger Williams. Their actions took a career criminal off the streets but the media did not see it that way. They saw it as the use of excessive force and the county prosecutor's office agreed. A number of cops were disciplined and the patrolman who fired the most shots was indicted on two counts of voluntary manslaughter.

I wonder how this story would have played out if Russell had run over a couple of black kids playing in the street during the police chase. Would he have received the same amount of sympathy from the black community? I doubt it.

We can debate whether the police acted properly or not until the cows come home. But I want to share with you the side story also by *Plain Dealer* reporter John Caniglia. Here's the headline: "Documents Paint Picture of Pair's History, Families." My observations below are edited from his story. The victim's stories give the reader a close look inside the BSC that our mainstream media seldom reports upon.

Let's look at the Williams family first. Caniglia reports that her mother, Martha Mae Williams, will receive $869,315 after the lawyers get their cut. Five aunts and uncles will get the rest. But her sister, Tiani Williams, 30, doesn't seem to be receiving anything to relieve her grief. Why not?

Because she is serving life in prison for killing her boyfriend after an argument. Prosecutors said she burned down her apartment while he was passed out in it. (More on this type of BSC behavior in my chapter on the Cleveland Fire Department.)

Malissa Williams also had her share of problems. Records indicate she had 33 dealings with the Cleveland Police Department since 2001, mostly for drug and mental health issues. Her attorney said she suffered from numerous incidents of domestic abuse and grappled with drug addiction.

Her sister, Tiani, the arsonist, also suffered from drug addiction and mental health issues. Records indicate she was abused as a child and as an adult. I wouldn't doubt that Malissa was also. No wonder Malissa Williams hooked up with the likes of Timothy Russell. A report stated she was living in a women's shelter and jumped in Russell's car to buy some drugs.

I feel sorry for both these ladies. They each had a tough life growing up in the middle of the BSC. But it is the BSC that is the problem. It is producing more and more of these kinds of children every day and it has to stop. But the only way to stop it is to pull it up by its roots.

We are rewarding Mom Williams with a huge sum of cash while we are trying to put a hard-working cop in jail. What kind of country have we created?

Someone should research these sisters' upbringing to try to understand why they had such a tough childhood. It is probably not that different from thousands of other black Cleveland kids in our inner cities. Were they raised on welfare? Did their father ever help support them? These are questions that are never asked in the media or academia. Like I said before, it is up to the reader to connect the dots.

Now let's turn our attention to Timothy Russell. He was a career criminal. Police records show he was arrested on charges of criminal trespassing, domestic violence, endangering children, petty theft, receiving stolen property, aggravated robbery, fleeing and eluding, and failure to comply with police. Sounds like he's been down the police chase route before. How would you like to see him racing past your front yard at 100 MPH while your children are outside playing on the lawn? Our black leaders never address this issue when discussing his case.

How would you like to have him as your next door neighbor? Why is he even out on the streets of our city with his criminal record? Easy. Because our jails are overcrowded with hundreds of others just like him. It is the BSC gone wild. His father is also going to receive a nice chunk of our tax money. What was that jury thinking?

Before we move on to the Tamir Rice case I would like my readers to once again think about the three-million-dollar settlement price tag for this case and what we could do with that kind of money. I mentioned earlier that we could use it to hire a bunch of new cops. It seems the city was already planning on doing just that. Here's the scoop from another *Plain Dealer* article from October 1, 2014.

The Federal Government is giving the city of Cleveland a $1.9 million dollar grant to hire 15 cops for three years. It is our part of a $124 million dollar national program. This is another one of President Obama's band aid solutions to our inner city crime problems.

Yet one of Cleveland's most outspoken black councilmen, Zack Reed, says it is not nearly enough. He claims the city needs to hire 185 more cops to "combat the city's epidemic of violence" (He'll never call it the BSC but that is what he is talking about.)

Let's do the math. If it costs $1.9 million to hire 15 cops it would cost about $24 million to hire 185 cops. And that's only for three years. What happens after three years? Do we lay off the cops and let the BSC go crazy again? Ask all the members of the BSC that don't pay any taxes to start kicking in? Ask the Williams family to kick in part of their settlement? Not going to happen.

So what did the cops on the street learn from this incident? Sadly, the same thing that the criminals on the street learned. That the thugs won. The next time a hardened criminal is pulled over for a traffic stop and wants to flee for his life why not let him go? Why put your career at risk to chase him? Let him run loose and terrorize his neighborhood. Is that what our black leaders really want?

The whole thing reminds me of my early cab driving career. Some black leaders back then were complaining that the cabbies were discriminating against blacks because they didn't like to pick up fares in the black neighborhoods.

As a young and dumb, fresh-out-of-college part-time cabbie I was one of the few who did. And you know who were the most vocal about telling me I was crazy for doing it? The black cab drivers. They said I was nuts. And do you want to know why? They told me that there was a good chance that when I ventured into the BSC neighborhood with my pockets full of cash that I might be robbed of my day's earnings.

I hope you are finally beginning to understand what I mean when I say the BSC is bankrupting our nation. I hope I am beginning to make some sense to my readers.

Am I being a racist when I declare that it is about time to change and even eliminate the BSC? I don't think so. It is time for our black leaders to stand up like real men and confront the real causes of the chaos in their communities. It is time for them to take a good look in their mirrors.

I hope you are beginning to see in how many different ways the BSC costs all of us huge sums of money.

Russell and Williams met receiving free meals at a Catholic hunger center. They both lived in free homeless shelters. They cost taxpayers thousands of dollars in welfare costs and charity donations. And then after they go on a wild goose chase, putting the lives of hundreds of Cleveland citizens, mostly black children, in danger, they cost us millions of dollars in court costs and settlement fees.

I have a crazy idea. How about charging the parents of Timothy and Malissa for all the money their children have cost the taxpayers of Cuyahoga County, Ohio, over the years? Maybe repay those expenses from their settlement awards? Yeah, like that one's going to fly.

Fast forward to a Tuesday May 5, 2015 story in the *Plain Dealer* by Cory Shaffer. He reports that: "Two teenagers robbed a woman of her purse and cellphone at gunpoint on Starkweather Avenue..." The police gave chase and once again the criminals sped away going about 100 MPH.

But because of the Williams/Russell case the police supervisor called off the chase and let the hoodlums get away.

Shaffer quoted the reaction of Steve Loomis, president of the Cleveland Police Patrolman's Association.

"They should have let us do our job," Loomis said. "These two punks will rob again, and what's even worse, they will tell their punk friends how easy it is to do in Cleveland."

Like I said, the thugs won.

Now let's see what we can learn from the other national case from Cleveland, Ohio. The Tamir Rice shooting.

A pair of Cleveland cops are patrolling the Cudell neighborhood on Cleveland's west side. It is very near to where I went to high school. When I was in school, forty years ago, it was a prosperous middle class neighborhood.

Today it is under the control of the BTC. It has a very nice rec center and swimming pool that serves as a gathering place for the BTC.

The two policemen receive a call on their radio that a black youth is threatening civilians by pointing a gun at cars driving by the rec center. The man who called the police told the dispatcher that "it might be a fake gun" but the police dispatcher never told that to the police officers.

When the two white cops pull up they don't know what's going on. They see a black youth pointing a gun at pedestrians. They tell him to drop the gun and when he doesn't do it the rookie cop shoots and kills him.

Tragically it is later discovered that the youth with the gun, Tamir Rice, is only twelve years old and was pointing a toy gun. The national media loves this story, just another example of white cops killing innocent black kids. Just another example of police brutality and racism. They neglect to examine some important facts to the story. Here are some things they should have considered.

The media and his relatives both portray Tamir Rice as a "little boy" and "their baby." However, he weighed 195 pounds. That's about what I weigh and it took me six decades to add all this girth.

The gun he was pointing looked exactly like a real gun. Toy guns are supposed to have a bright-colored band around the handle to show they are not real but Tamir took it off. No one seems to know why. Even if he didn't, how are the cops supposed to spot the difference on the spur of the moment?

What are they supposed to say to someone who is pointing a gun at them? "Hey, buddy, is that a real gun or a toy gun that you are pointing at me?" That's the kind of policing that our U.S. Justice Department wants our inner city cops to practice. Crazy, eh?

Here's what bothers me most about the uproar that ensued over Tamir's tragic death. Once again the media and Barack Obama hooked it up with the same controversy surrounding the police shooting in Ferguson, Missouri. Maybe they should concentrate instead on how the BSC raises its children.

Let me first confess right here and now that I was no angel when I was growing up in the city of Cleveland. During my early teen years my friends and I roamed the streets much like Tamir and company. We were not in any gangs but we did like to play pranks, much like in the movie *American Graffiti*.

But they were innocent pranks just going for some laughs. I cannot imagine any of us waking up on a Saturday morning and telling ourselves, "I think I'll take my toy gun over to the rec center and scare the crap out of a bunch of white people."

Like I addressed earlier, we also used to fight quite a bit in my youth. It must have been the testosterone acting up. But we settled our differences with our fists and the next day we were friends again. No one ever pulled out a gun or a knife.

This is why the BTC is a whole different ball game. Black thugs will pull out a gun at the drop of a hat. And after the smoke clears there is no room left to make up the next day.

So let's take a look at Tamir Rice's neighborhood. On Wednesday, November 26, 2014 the *Plain Dealer's* front page headline was: "DEMONSTRATORS SHUT DOWN SHOREWAY, Protests Decry Fatal Police Shootings of Black Youths in Cleveland, Ferguson." On the same front page was another story that I found infinitely more interesting.

The headline said TAMIR'S NEIGHBORHOOD PLAGUED BY GANGS AND GUNS. Right there it tells me Tamir Rice's Cudell neighborhood bore no resemblance to the Cudell neighborhood I knew when I was in high school.

PD reporter Cory Shaffer interviewed people who live in the area and studied police records. He said the history of the Cudell Park neighborhood is "marred by violence ... The Park is the epicenter, long plagued by gangs, guns and drugs."

Just with that statement alone he illustrates everything I have been saying about what happens when the BTC infects a neighborhood. Here are some other random excerpts from his story to prove my point. I will edit them for brevity.

Graffiti covers almost every surface in sight.

A mechanic shop nestled between crumbling warehouses warns customers that the business is not responsible for vehicle fires, break-ins or smashed windows.

A once notorious gang waged a "reign of terror" ... BBE 900 as an off-shoot of the larger Heartless Felons gang.

A county prosecutor explained that: "The BBE 900 gang bragged that they owned the streets and demonstrated the ability to assault or steal from whomever they found."

"A grand jury dealt a blow to the gang last month by handing up a 299-count indictment against 38 people—including 26 juveniles—on charges connected to killings, shootings and assaults, robberies, kidnappings, burglaries and break-ins in the neighborhood.

A resident "acknowledged that his neighborhood is troubled, citing open drug dealings and stick-ups. It's tough with people going around jumping and robbing people."

Another resident who just moved back to the Cudell neighborhood recalled what it was like when he lived there five years ago. He said he watched drug deals made in daylight and gun shots on nearby streets

were second nature. "I left because of all the trouble... it was crazy." But
it is worse now, he said.

See what I mean by a BTC neighborhood? The citizens should be begging the cops to crack down on the thugs. But when they do, what happens? All hell breaks loose against them.

How would you like to live in this kind of neighborhood? Are you beginning to understand what "white flight" is all about? Do you even have a clue as to what Cleveland cops must put up with on a daily basis?

But before I finish discussing the BTC and the CPD there is one more interesting fact that the national media forgets to mention when talking about the Tamir Rice incident.

In that same Cudell Park there are two markers honoring two Cleveland police officers who were killed by suspects in the same neighborhood. In 1996 a drug dealer killed Detective Robert Clark in the stairwell of a nearby apartment building. And a rape suspect shot Detective Jonathan Schroeder in 2006 as he tried to arrest him in a nearby home.

Makes you pause for a moment, does it not? Any wonder that a cop comes out shooting when confronted by someone holding a gun, no matter what their age? All these Monday morning quarterbacks sit in their nice suburban homes and newspaper offices and like to second-guess what the cops should do. Have any of them ever had a gun pointed at them? I think not.

So I ask you a second time, what have the police and criminals learned from all the hoopla over this second incident of a white cop shooting a black suspect? That the thugs won again.

If you are a cop why do anything anymore? Forget about racing to the scene when a black youth is threatening residents with a gun. Just wait until he shoots a few of them first. Then show up and do a couple of reports. The odds of going home alive are much greater anyway.

And what do our black president, Barack Obama, and our black Attorney General, Eric Holder, say is the solution to all our police problems? To better train the police. Wow, what a great idea.

A *Plain Dealer* story by Rich Exner on June 3, 2015 estimates the cost of the latest Consent Decree "will run into the millions—each year, for several years running."

They based their estimate on the costs of similar Consent Decrees in other cities. "In New Orleans, the cost over five years is expected to total $55 million."

For what? So we can retrain our veteran cops on how to be tree huggers? Let them learn from Obama's example about how to deal with international terrorists? (Sorry, off the subject, but I couldn't resist that zinger.)

As soon as I heard the term "Consent Decree" I knew we were in trouble. Consent Decrees were used to justify Affirmative Action and school busing. Where is the city of Cleveland supposed to find all this money? Take it from the Fire Department and the Streets Department? We wouldn't need all these expensive "reforms" if the cops did not have to deal with the BTC in the first place.

A lot of insiders are going to make a lot of money while our police departments go to crap just like our big city schools. The federal government likes to tell local municipalities what to do but they never seem to figure out how to pay for their fancy ideas.

Most of our local black leaders agree that we must change the police culture, it is the source of all our inner city problems. Attorney General Eric Holder spent a great amount of money and energy to tell us how Cleveland's cops are a bunch of racist pigs. Even Cleveland's African American Ministers Leadership Council gave our BLACK mayor and our BLACK police chief a list of demands for reforming the Cleveland police department.

My argument is that instead of changing the police culture it is time to change the inner city Black Subculture, the BSC. We would save a lot more money in the long run. And it seems that our nation's first African American President, Barack Obama, might actually agree with me.

In an op-ed piece in the *Plain Dealer* on May 1, 2015, Ramesh Ponnuru, a columnist for *Bloomberg View*, gave us President Obama's take on the Baltimore Freddie Gray riots.

Ponnuru wrote that Obama "made the case that the police alone can't solve the problems of 'communities where there are no fathers who can provide guidance to young men; communities where there's no investment and manufacturing has been stripped away; and drugs have flooded the community.'"

I am glad that President Obama agrees with my assessment of the Black Subculture. But what has he done to improve it in six years as president? The dirty little secret of the Democratic Party is that it needs to keep the BSC dependent on the Federal Government so they will keep voting for the Democratic Party.

The big difference between President Obama and me is in how to fix the mess our inner cities find themselves in. As a liberal Democrat he proposes more costly government programs like the ones that got us here in the first place. As a conservative Republican I say get the government the hell out of our lives and quit subsidizing unwed black mothers with our tax money.

Isn't it about time we changed the conversation about race in America? Is anyone out there listening?

The other solution our fearless leaders like Obama and Holder propose is to make all cops wear body cameras so we can second-guess every move they make all day long. Give the Monday morning quarterbacks more info to talk about on the 24-hour news programs.

Isn't that wonderful? Are Obama and Holder going to wear body cameras also? Why shouldn't they? They are public servants on the taxpayers' dime just like the cops. Don't we have the right to see what they do with our money all day also?

The same goes for all our mayors, councilmen and members of the U.S. Congress. They are all public servants.

And what are they going to show the public about a big city cop's typical day in the BSC neighborhoods? Are they going to let the taxpayers see all the crap a Cleveland cop has to put up with during his daily tour of duty? I seriously doubt it.

I wish I was wearing a body camera during the 20 years I served in BSC hoods as a city of Cleveland fire fighter. I could make a documentary out of it and call it "Folks Acting Like Fools." No one would believe it was for real. They would think it was science fiction.

But I didn't have one so instead you'll just have to read my next chapter, "The BSC and the Cleveland Fire Department (CFD)."

CHAPTER TWELVE:
THE BSC AND THE CFD

I HAVE SO many stories about the Black Subculture from my 32-year career as a city of Cleveland fire fighter that I do not even know where to begin. So let me begin at the beginning.

My first day on the Cleveland Fire Department I went to four house fires. The year was 1982 and Cleveland's predominantly black east side was losing homes to fires at an alarming rate. Some called it urban renewal. Twenty years later when I finally transferred to Cleveland's west side, many of the east side neighborhoods I worked in looked like Germany or Japan after World War II. There would be maybe one or two houses left on a street.

We put our lives in danger every day putting out all the fires but the media barely noticed unless someone died or was injured or it was a big old abandoned factory. Sadly, there were a lot of those on Cleveland's east side also.

The homes were older and many were in disrepair but they weren't any older than the same style homes on the city's predominately white west side which had barely any fires.

What was the difference in the two sides of the city? The BSC factor, that's what. What I am trying to show you here is that the BSC factor must be considered no matter what the subject.

My fire station was in the Hough neighborhood. The Hough riots of 1966 gained national attention just like Watts. Like many inner city black neighborhoods across the country in the 1960s, Hough residents torched their own homes and businesses to protest racial discrimination and redlining. Sound familiar?

One of my favorite stories from the Hough riots was from an older fireman who was still on the job when I started. He was a black fireman and he was shot at while sitting in the back of the fire truck. The bullets went through the metal door and almost killed him. You should hear his opinion of his fellow black rioters. A little too politically incorrect to repeat here. These are the types of stories the media and academia neglect to tell.

Back to redlining. That was the practice where banks didn't give out many loans in the black areas of the city. There was a reason for that. Thanks to the BSC the neighborhoods were trashed and their home values were plummeting. So what bank would want to give out a loan to an area that is dropping in value? Chances are you were not going to be repaid. It is not a good business practice. But blacks claimed they were being discriminated against and the federal government stepped in and forced banks to make such loans. This was one of the main causes of what Barack Obama calls the "Great Recession of 2008" but neither the media nor academia dare to mention it.

But I digress. More on the Great Recession later. When I joined the Cleveland Fire Department in the early 1980s it was considered one of the finest fire departments in the country. "The best fire department between Chicago and New York City," the old timers would tell us. And they were right. Want to know why?

Very simple. We had a lot of practice. We put out a lot of house fires. And we had tough hiring standards. (More about that in the Affirmative Action chapter.) During my first twenty years on the department I worked in numerous BSC neighborhoods. I learned about my fellow black citizens and their culture, up close and personal. I went into their homes when they caught on fire or when a resident was having a heart attack or a drug overdose. And we were busy, very busy.

My first ten years on the job we went to a house fire almost every shift we worked. That was our normal routine. You came to work in the morning and you knew you were probably going to have a house fire sometime during your 24-hour shift. (That is how I could work as a part-time cab driver on my day off.) Sometimes we would have a fire in the morning, sometimes in the afternoon, sometimes in the evening, sometimes all three times. It was an exciting time to be a big city fire fighter.

But what, you may ask, was going on in these black neighborhoods to cause all these fires? A number of factors were at work. First, many of them were caused by the BSC lifestyle. Often a resident would fall asleep after drinking too much alcohol or overdosing on drugs while leaving the stove on or a candle lit.

Some of my most tragic fires were caused by burning cigarettes. We once lost five children at a fire when a resident fell asleep with a lit cigarette on their couch. It was only a couch fire and we put it out quickly. But as we worked the hose line from room to room we kept stumbling on sleeping kids who died from the smoke inhalation. It was terribly sad.

The other big factor was arson fires. Many of these homes were rental properties and their mortgages were underwater. While real estate values were booming in much of our nation, BSC neighborhood values were going in the other direction.

Landlords discovered that their homes were much more valuable to the insurance companies than to their renters. It was more profitable to burn them down than to maintain them. They wanted to get their investment out of their properties before they became worthless.

Also, many blacks set their own homes on fire. It was an easy way to escape the BSC neighborhood filled with crime and drugs and prostitution. If you owned your home you could use the insurance money as a down payment on another house in a better neighborhood. If you were a renter you could escape your rental contract and the CMHA would give you another Section 8 subsidy in another hopefully better neighborhood. Either way it was an upgrade of lifestyle. The problem is that once too many Section 8 residents moved into a new neighborhood, that one would begin to flip and home values would begin to plummet. The same cycle of crime, drugs and prostitution would reappear.

It is that never-ending cycle that I warned you about at the beginning of this book.

Oh, and I almost forgot the other reason for arson fires. Where most of them were set in empty houses, some were set for more sinister motives. These were much more stressful for us because we not only had to try to save the house but also save the residents trapped inside.

Sometimes our BSC residents would use fire as a weapon. That was an inner city choice of violent behavior. The motives were often jealousy, revenge or just plain hatred. (See the Tiani Williams story in the CPD chapter.)

Myself and three fellow firemen almost died trying to save the occupants at a motel fire. It was started by a prostitute who got mad at her pimp and set his bed on fire. When it was over the four-story building was left with only three stories.

So what did I learn from working 20 years in a BSC community? How was it different than the white neighborhoods where I lived and grew up?

First of all, the biggest and most important difference is the lack of fathers in the homes we visited. We actually go inside our citizens' homes for any number of reasons. Maybe someone would be having a heart attack or a diabetic emergency. We would show up and stabilize the patient until an ambulance arrived to transport them to hospital. Sometimes we would deliver babies that would not wait until their mom made it to the hospital. Other times we would install free smoke detectors, a service we provided to all the citizens of Cleveland.

But the one common thread of all our visits was the lack of adult males. They are practically non-existent among the BSC, unless we were responding to a gunshot wound or knifing but that's another story. Sometimes there would be an older couple, like my parents' age, from the WWII generation. Then we might see an adult male with his elderly wife. But otherwise forget about it.

The typical modern BSC family unit that we dealt with was a single mom, maybe with a couple of her female friends, and a bunch of little rug rats who paid the bills by just existing. Dependent children have replaced male adults as the bread winners in the BSC communities. It is the BSC formula for economic success. Who would invent such a system? It needs to change if our country ever wants to heal its racial and economic wounds.

The second big difference between the BSC communities I worked in and the white communities I lived in was the overall physical environment. Trash and litter were common always and everywhere in the east side neighborhoods. Yet in the lower and middle class white neighborhoods where I grew up litter and trash were pretty much non-existent.

What's the difference? Very simple. If I see some trash or litter in my hood I pick it up. So do my neighbors. It is the way I learned from my elders. My grandparents lived in an old Cleveland neighborhood that was about the same age as the Hough neighborhood I worked in. But they always kept their yard and house immaculate. I followed their example. What kind of example do these BSC moms show their kids? They expect the government to do everything for them.

Often when white suburbanites visited our fire station they would always look around and say: "Someone should do something about all this trash." Someone always means "the government." No one ever holds the BSC responsible for its own environment.

City workers would occasionally clean up the streets but the trash would always somehow mysteriously reappear. Our standing joke was that a bunch of rich suburban white kids must have snuck into the neighborhood under the cover of darkness and dumped it all.

Poverty is always the BSC's excuse for their anti-social behavior but my parents and grandparents were dirt poor and they never used it as an excuse for anything. They cleaned up their own properties. And they maintained them.

This is another big problem in the BSC hoods. There is very little maintenance being done on the homes or the yards. It is a problem shared by our government entities at all levels.

The second fire station that I worked at was in an outlying east side neighborhood. The BSC was just beginning to move in. Driving along the streets it looked like a nice middle class neighborhood. But when we stopped and checked the fire hydrants we had a closer look at the homes. Then I noticed the changes occurring, the paint peeling and the roof tiles missing. The white citizens who were just moving out left their homes in excellent physical shape. But on closer inspection they were already showing signs of neglect. I visited that neighborhood again later in my career and it was a real tragedy. The houses were falling apart. They say it takes a village to raise a child. It takes about one generation to trash a neighborhood.

This is why, just like the Hough neighborhood, it would eventually be called a "ghetto." Once again their excuse is that they don't own the homes, so they expect their landlords to do everything for them. But why would the landlords care as long as the government keeps the Section 8 money flowing? There was no incentive for it. Once again the government was expected to solve a problem that it created in the first place.

In contrast I had a lot of friends from West Tech High School who rented their inner city homes similar to the ones in the BSC neighborhoods. But they used their own hard-earned money to pay the rent. And they worked with their landlords to paint and maintain their homes, inside and outside, as a matter of pride.

Enough on those subjects. I am sure that you already feel that I am a racist bigot and I am just feeding your opinion. But I am just sharing with you my honest observations.

When I went to the west side to put out fires my job became much easier. I was reminded of a suburban fireman I met off the job. He worked in a middle class white suburb. I was curious about his career. After a while he admitted to me that in 30 years as a suburban fire fighter he never went to a house fire.

I was in shock but then I realized that is a good thing. It means the residents take care of their property. Some folks would argue that he did not earn his salary but you have to understand that the fire department is like the insurance policy on your house and car. You have to have one and it is great to have one when you need it but isn't it better if you never have to use it? Besides, suburban firemen do all the medical runs that we Cleveland guys never had the time for. That's why in the city of Cleveland we had a separate division called the Emergency Medical Service (EMS). They ran the ambulances because we were too busy putting out fires.

There is one last difference that I noticed after I transferred to the white west side of Cleveland. It was the way the residents treat the firemen and their neighbors.

I could tell you lots of stories but you probably wouldn't believe most of them. But if you ever have the opportunity to talk with any big city cop or fireman I am sure they could bend your ear with many unbelievable tales.

Here's just a small sample. It happened more than once in my career. Sometimes we would return to our east side fire station after spending a couple of hours putting out a house fire. And what would we find? That some of our neighbors tried to steal our cars or tried to break into the fire station so they could rob us. That is the BSC at its finest. That was the thanks we would get for putting our lives on the line for the community.

So many times I would see brave firemen do risky things in the line of duty, take chances they did not have to take for the sake of protecting our citizens' lives and property. It was the kind of stuff that did not show up on the 11 o'clock news but it made me proud of my profession.

But in my 20 years of serving the black community I seldom heard a "thank you" from a black city resident after putting out a fire. Instead they usually had some kind of complaint as a "taxpayer," like: "Where's the Red Cross?"

Meanwhile on the white west side the residents would not only thank us for our efforts but offer us a cup of coffee or a bottle of water.

And you wonder why cops or firemen or teachers who have to deal with the BSC on a daily basis cop an attitude? What would you do?

Before we move on there was one more issue raised in *Plain Dealer* reporter John Caniglia's story about Malissa Williams that we discussed in the previous chapter. Malissa was the lady shot 137 times by Cleveland cops after a police chase through our fair city. I would like to address it while I have the opportunity. I think they will provide you with even more insight into the BSC.

It seems that after word of her relatives receiving a cash settlement from the city hit the streets, four people showed up claiming to be Williams's half-siblings. DNA tests proved they were not. This is also typical.

For example, in the white community, if a bus crashes into a car or a pole on the city's streets, the neighbors come out of their homes to help the victims. In the black community everyone jumps on the bus pretending to be passengers in hopes of a earning a cash settlement from Cleveland's Regional Transit Authority. Once again, I could not make this stuff up. What a difference in cultures. (SSDAS).

Next up, I'm going to look at racism within the Cleveland Fire Department, but this is not what you expect. It is black racism that I am talking about and it is called Affirmative Action.

CHAPTER THIRTEEN: AFFIRMATIVE ACTION

BEFORE I BEGIN my explanation of Affirmative Action (AA) let me share with you a couple of thoughts that have been twirling around in my head since I first experienced AA up close and personal. I will tell you all you need to know about Affirmative Action and how it works. Very simply, AA is about putting unqualified African Americans in positions of responsibility because their people were somehow discriminated against sometime in the far and distant past.

Here we go. This is what I firmly believe based on my experience with Affirmative Action:

If we had AA during World War II, we would all be doing the Nazi goosestep during our annual holiday parades. If we had AA during the space race with Russia during the Cold War, we would still be trying to figure out how to land on the moon. And if President Barack Obama is applying AA to our military, like he seems to be doing to the rest of the federal government, then that explains why we cannot win a war against a country called ISIS that is about the size of Pennsylvania and doesn't even have a navy or an air force.

Let me first confess that I have met a large number of racists during my thirty-plus-year career on the Cleveland Fire Department. But sadly, most of them were black firemen.

The white firemen had good reason to be upset having to deal with the fallout of Affirmative Action hiring but when push came to shove they realized that the hiring process was out of their hands. A federal judge decreed it and they would have to live with it. All they really wanted from the black AA firemen was that they show up on time and do their job. Is that too much to ask?

Most white people have not experienced racial discrimination up close and personal. Lucky for them. So before I explain to you how affirmative action works I must do a "full disclosure." I have been "diversified." In other words I have been a victim of racial discrimination. Others call it "reverse discrimination." I call it "black racism."

Actually I was "diversified" even before I was hired but I did not know it at the time. My main case of discrimination came much later in my career when I applied for a transfer from my busy east side fire station to a much quieter station on the city's west side. I already explained the differences in the previous chapters so let me start there first.

I spent twenty years putting out fires in the BSC neighborhood and it was time to move on. My body was taking a beating. I wasn't getting any younger and I still had three young children to raise. Besides, that was the way the fire department operated. You learned the trade on the busy east side and then after earning your stripes you transitioned into a quieter fire station later in your career.

The whole move was governed by union rules. When a fireman retires, his spot is open to bids. The fireman with the most seniority who bids on the spot gets it. But not when race is an issue. Instead, our black fire chief gave the spot I applied for to a black fireman with much less seniority than me. A fireman who never spent much time in the trenches, so to speak. He did not earn the sweet spot on the west side like I did. It was kind of like how Section 8 housing works.

Wouldn't you think that the black fireman would want to work in a neighborhood where he could help his black brothers and sisters? Of course not. Wonder why? Did you read my chapter on the Black Subculture? That's the easy answer. His action kind of reminded me of our professional athlete class. How many of our black athletes move into a black neighborhood after signing a million-dollar contract? Not many, I can assure you. (SSDAS)

Back to my transfer denial. Our black chief said he gave my spot to a black fireman in the name of "diversity."

When I complained to the union about it they said that when it came to "diversity" I didn't have much hope in filing a grievance that union rules were broken. The union rep reminded me of the cop at my grandma's house who told me that if it was my word against the black lady's, I was going to lose.

When is this stuff ever going to end? I had been paying union dues for union jobs since I was 16 and I never filed a grievance in my life. Now the one time I really have a case they tell me to forget it.

Because of my seniority I was already working the position in question as a temporary fill-in until it was officially posted. So when the much younger black guy came to replace me I took his picture with my camera.

He became upset and asked me what I was doing. I told him that I was going to take the picture home and show it to my kids so that when they learn about "Affirmative Action" in school they will know what it looks like. The funny thing is that they probably don't teach it in our schools because it is "black racism" pure and simple and black racism is politically incorrect.

My case was only a small example but it is interesting how members of a race that have complained about "discrimination" their entire lives have no qualms about doing it themselves when they are able to do so.

To be honest, my diversification was not very traumatic. Compared to all the other racial problems on the Cleveland Fire Department it was not that big of a deal. For me it was just a matter of principle.

However, to many other firemen who were victims of Affirmative Action it could be a life changer, especially when it came to promotions. You see, an unqualified black fireman could actually take the promotion from a white fireman who scored much higher than him on the promotional test. This could cost a white fireman hundreds of thousands of dollars over the course of his career. This made a lot of white firemen angry and bitter.

Just so I do not make this too complicated to understand, let me go back to the beginning of my career and explain to you about Affirmative Action and government civil service tests.

Affirmative Action (AA) is racism on a grand scale. Quite simply the government started a program where race was used to hire and promote employees instead of more important qualifications like intelligence and strength. And just like school busing AA was unconstitutional.

Once again, just like school busing, AA was mandated by federal judges who overstepped their judicial authority. Someone would complain about the number of blacks on a job and a judge would order a "consent decree" which is actually a code word for "racial quotas."

When I first became a city of Cleveland fireman, AA was just beginning on the Cleveland Fire Department (CFD). A federal judge had ordered that the city hire more black firemen regardless of where they placed on the civil service test. But our union, Local 93 of the International Association of Fire Fighters (IAFF), was fighting against its implementation because it was blatantly unfair. In fact, Local 93 took our grievance all the way to the Supreme Court. We were the test case for Affirmative Action and we lost. The times and the court were stacked against our union even though our argument made perfect sense.

Here was our argument. We took a tough competitive civil service test to become firemen. Why don't they just hire the citizens who scored the highest on the test?

Instead, the fire department was under orders by the federal government to hire more black firemen, qualifications be damned. I did not realize it at the time but AA affected me from the day I took the civil service entrance exam.

As I mentioned in a previous chapter, the CFD had tough hiring standards. Over 3000 applicants took the test which consisted of a mental test and a physical test. The physical test had a long tradition in the fire service. We had to perform a few strenuous tasks like raising a ladder to a two-story window and dragging a hose line between markers. Not only did we have to do it, we were tested on how fast we did it. The test was developed to find candidates who were scholarly athletes, firemen who could perform tough physical feats with enough sense to make wise choices at a fire scene.

And the system worked fine until the federal government threw Affirmative Action into the mix.

Here's how AA worked. A few seconds difference on our test scores greatly influenced our rankings. So did missing one or two questions on the mental exam. After all the results were in we were each given a number. For instance, if you ranked number ten out of 3000 applicants there was a good chance you were going to be hired. If you ranked 1000 your chances were pretty slim. Unless you were an African American.

Fortunately, at the time I took the exam, many of the World War II generation firemen were beginning to retire. Over the next few years the city would need over 300 new firemen to replace them. Still, ranking in the top 300 out of 3000 in a very competitive test was difficult to say the least. I didn't realize it until I was hired but my ranking was also influenced by my race.

What happened is that black applicants that scored behind my ranking were hired before me. So by the time they got to my number a lot of black guys who scored worse than me were already hired. In fact, some of them scored a lot worse.

What it came down to was that the white guys were competing against the white guys and the black guys were competing against the black guys. For the black guys the standards were a heck of a lot lower, kind of like lowering the bar for graduation in the Cleveland public school system.

I was lucky to even get the job. I was one of the last guys hired off the list. Right after my number there were a lot of poor white guys who should have been hired because of their ranking but were replaced by black guys who scored worse than them.

Those guys lost a great career opportunity because of reverse discrimination. And then it happened to me all over again when it came time for a promotion. Once again black firemen were given promotions even though they scored lower on a promotional civil service exam.

The first time I took a test for lieutenant they promoted a bunch of black guys who scored lower than me on the promotional exam. Then they killed the list, which means they ran out of open lieutenant spots to fill. I would have to wait a few more years to take the exam again.

Meanwhile the newly-minted black AA lieutenants could take the test for the next rank of captain. And be given another free promotion. With each promotion up the ladder to lieutenant, captain, battalion chief and assistant chief comes a pay raise. So thanks to Affirmative Action, a white guy who lost a promotion that he deserved to be a lieutenant also lost his chance to advance in rank and move up the pay scale.

Some guys lost numerous promotions to AA black firemen throughout their career even though they outscored them on every test they took. That's why I said a white fireman could have lost hundreds of thousands of dollars over a typical thirty-year career.

The AA process caused a lot of racial animosity among the ranks of firemen. I've been told by the older guys that they had no problem getting along with the black fireman who worked with them because they actually earned their stripes. So once again the federal government stepped in and caused more racial problems instead of solving them.

And you wonder why our union fought it all the way to the Supreme Court. If the judges followed the law they would have told the lower courts to stay out of the hiring process. Instead they threw the white firemen under the bus. They followed the mantra of the times that argued that the "government approved minority," African Americans, deserved special treatment because their ancestors were slaves a hundred years ago. (The Cleveland police force was going through the same process.)

This was another idea brought to you by John F. Kennedy's "best and brightest." They didn't care about the white guys who were unfairly shut out of an occupation. None of their kids wanted to be cops or firemen, so who cares? Anyone could do that job, right?

What you ended up with was a bunch of unqualified black cops and firemen. The idea behind AA was to create a black middle class. But just as school busing was used to upgrade their schools and Section 8 gave them a free upgrade in their housing, the "government approved minority" did not have to earn their positions like white people do. They were just handed to them on a platter. Same with their promotions.

Just take a black guy off the streets of Cleveland who barely graduated from high school and put him in charge of a half-a-million-dollar fire truck and three other firemen. Or give a borderline criminal a gun and a badge and make him a cop. It was after they lowered the hiring standards that the Cleveland police department began having its own problems.

You should have seen some of the black firemen who were hired under our AA court order. Just the ones off my hiring list make an interesting study. (SSDAS) First, let me make one thing perfectly clear. It is very hard to be fired from a government position. You basically have to commit a felony or worse. And the sad part is all the white guys who were left sitting at home without jobs that were taken by black guys who were eventually fired.

There were black firemen off my hiring list fired for all kinds of reasons, like dealing drugs or stealing from the other firemen. Then there were the ones who were killed off the job by their girlfriends or angry renters.

There were so many stories and it was so long ago that I forget a lot of the details. But they were all part of the BSC lifestyle. Are these the type of fireman you want coming into your home when your mom has a heart attack? Or your sister is delivering a premature baby? I sure as hell wouldn't want them in my house taking care of my family. But a federal judge says: "Don't worry about it, anyone can do your job." Thank you, JFK's "whiz kids."

Now if you are a thinking person maybe you would ask yourself this question: Shouldn't these guys have had some sort of background check or something? You would think.

But thanks to Affirmative Action a lot of the previous standards were lowered. Which brings us to an interesting coincidence.

Remember the Tamir Rice case about the rookie white cop killing the twelve-year-old black kid who was waving around a toy gun that looked real? The media discovered that there were some questions about his hiring in the first place. It seems he had some problems with guns at a previous police job. The black community wanted to know why he was hired with such a background.

Maybe it all goes back to the city's love affair with Affirmative Action. AA lowered the bar for black police candidates so the same standards applied to the white ones. You heard it here first. You're not going to hear it from anyone else in the media, but I believe we need to connect the dots between the Tamir Rice case and Affirmative Action. Someone should look into it.

Now let's take a quick look at the lawsuits that were a direct result of Affirmative Action. A number of the black firemen were crazy about suing everyone. They would have five or six discrimination lawsuits going on at the same time against different cities. Just like the black railroaders, they were tying up the justice system with frivolous lawsuits.

Why not? It does not cost them anything. Let the lawyers do the work, throw enough crap against the wall and if something sticks, the lawyer gets his cut and the black fireman hauls in some nice cash without lifting a finger. All you need is a black judge and a black jury and everything falls nicely into place. Our justice system is crumbling and the cost to our local municipalities is enormous but who cares? (SSDAS)

I could give you tons of examples but here is my favorite. I explained that when we first came on the job we were very busy with fires. At one of the fire stations in one of Cleveland's worst neighborhoods there was a black fireman who refused to get off the fire truck when they pulled up at a fire. He would just sit in the fire truck until the fire was out but he was paid the same as the white guys who were putting their lives on the line every day.

Discipline him, you say? You would think. If we were in the Army he would be court-martialed. But in the AA environment it was almost impossible for a white officer to discipline a black fireman without cries of discrimination from the Vanguards, the local black firemen's union. (Yes, blacks have their own fire union while at the same time being members of our union, kind of like double dipping.)

So his white fellow firemen tried to shame him into doing his job. At a "working fire" you need as much manpower as possible. Since they were working shorthanded his actions were making their job even more dangerous than it already was.

So what happened? He played the race card. He sued the fire department for discrimination. And guess what? He won and went home with a big cash settlement.

How could that happen? Welcome to the world of Affirmative Action. I hope it never infects your job. Actually, maybe if it did affect more Americans they would understand better what AA is really all about.

Too hard to believe? That's just one example of the many problems we faced working in an AA fire department.

Here's one from my own career. Maybe it will seal the deal for you. When I was a lieutenant working on a pumper we pulled up on a commercial building fire. A couple other fire engines from another station were already on the scene. Our job as the second pumper on the scene was to help the first pumper supply water for the guys taking the fire hoses inside the building. But there was a problem. A couple of guys were trapped on the roof of the building and needed help. So I told the AA fireman who was driving our pumper to help me take a ladder off a different fire truck, a hook and ladder, so we could rescue the guys on the roof.

Do you know what he told me? "Not my job." Why? Because his job that day was to drive our pumper which he liked to do because that meant that he did not have to go inside the building and fight the fire. I didn't have time to argue with him so I went and found a couple other guys to help me raise a ladder to the roof of the building so the firemen could come down safely.

The fire department is a semi-military organization, especially on a fire scene. And the AA fireman disobeyed a direct order from a superior officer. Just like the other guy, he should have been court-martialed.

But when I tried to put him up on charges to discipline him, he played the race card. I'm suddenly being paid visits from lots of black AA members of the Vanguards, the black firemen's union.

I soon realized that disciplining the guy was not worth the trouble. I settled for a verbal apology. This was the new AA fire department. It reminded me of Cleveland's BSC school system.

I could tell you lots of similar stories but I don't have the time or the space to list them all here. Maybe some other time. (SSDAS) Instead we are going to inspect how AA created the black middle class.

CHAPTER FOURTEEN:
THE BLACK MIDDLE CLASS

OKAY, HERE WE GO again. Let's go back to why Affirmative Action was started in the first place. The idea was to help create a black middle class. Once again, while other "minorities" worked their way into the middle class, our "government approved minority," African Americans, wanted the government to help them out. And I could understand why.

When I would sit at my desk as a substitute teacher in the Cleveland public school system after it became mostly black kids, I would watch them in amazement. Oh, the things that I would see. Many of them stay with me still.

I remember the black girl who walked into the room and picked her textbook off her desk and slammed it to the ground screaming: "I don't need this shit." In my twelve years as a student I never saw anything even closely resembling this kind of behavior. It would have been the talk of the school for weeks. But in the BSC Cleveland schools it was not the least bit unusual or out of character. I figured she was just having a bad day so I left her alone.

On a typical day as a substitute, no matter what building I was in, I would sit at my desk and look through the door window and see lots of kids wandering the hallways who were supposed to be in a classroom but were not. Then I would look through the outside window and I would see lots of kids roaming outside on the school grounds who were supposed to be inside the building but were not. I would watch them wander into class late and then give me excuses to want to leave early. I would watch some of the ones who did show up in class just fell asleep out of the blue.

And I would wonder to myself: "Who would want to hire any of these kids?" They had a terrible work ethic. They didn't show up for class and if they did they would come in late. And they could hardly string a sentence together without dropping an "F bomb" or using the "N" word.

If I owned a business these would be the last kids on earth that I would consider hiring. I guess many employers feel the same way because unemployment in the BSC community is always much higher than in the rest of the country. Black leaders call it discrimination but I call it just good business sense.

One of the biggest reasons is the problem I outlined in the previous chapter on Affirmative Action. Once you hire an African American employee you cannot discipline them or, heaven forbid, fire them without their playing the race card. Then you have the NAACP and the U.S. Equal Employment Opportunity Commission (EEOC) on your back. So why go out asking for trouble in the first place?

That is why the federal government had to step in and force government agencies to hire African Americans. They came up with this idea of "racial quotas." If the city of Cleveland was 30 percent African American, it needed to have 30 percent of its employees African American. That makes absolutely no sense to me. It is just an easy argument for hiring more African Americans.

I never saw this argument used for other minorities. Like if the city is five percent Eskimo (a real minority), do we need five percent Eskimo firemen? Hell no.

This is why most white people argue that Affirmative Action is "reverse discrimination" or "black racism."

But AA did give many blacks their first introduction to the working world. And it is why most blacks now work for the government. If a private industry had to hire racial quotas it would most likely go out of business.

However, the argument has been applied to certain industries like the construction industry. Especially if they take government money or receive government tax breaks.

So our black Cleveland city council passed a law that requires any new building projects in Cleveland be made with a certain percentage of black workers. The law increases the cost of the project as companies must pay unskilled workers with few job skills. They must pay a guy who stands in traffic and holds up a stop sign the same rate as a guy pounding nails. Who comes up with this stuff?

THE dirty little secret of the black middle class is that it could not exist without the failures of the Black Subculture. How many black judges, cops, jailers and maintenance workers raised their families on the wages they earned dealing with the black criminal element?

How many black employees work for welfare agencies and housing projects and all the other government agencies whose main objective is to distribute free stuff to the BSC? Thousands.

While one half of the BSC is receiving billions of dollars in entitlements another half is receiving billions for administering all the entitlements. So instead of contributing to our nation's treasury the BSC is draining it dry.

Here's one of my favorites examples to show you what I mean by the double-edged sword that is bankrupting our nation.

On Friday April 3, 2015 there was a story in the *Plain Dealer* by Andrew Tobias headlined: BUDISH HIRES FORMER FOE TO HEAD COUNTY'S BENEFIT-OUTREACH EFFORTS.

Democrat Armond Budish is our newly elected Cuyahoga County Executive. (Almost all the politicians in Cuyahoga County and the city of Cleveland are Democrats, just like in all the big cities since the 1960s.)

Tobias explained that Budish intended to hire Marcia McCoy, a former political opponent, to fill a newly created position.

> "McCoy, 53, will receive $103,000 a year to work with community groups and the media to help eligible residents sign up for government benefits, something that Budish has identified as a priority of his administration."

The story goes on to explain that there might be some problems with McCoy double dipping. It becomes a big media story for a few days. Be that what it may.

What the media neglected to ask is why the county even created such a position in the first place. My problem with the hiring is why do they need to pay a black woman $103,000 a year to help other blacks register for more free stuff? Aren't they already getting everything they can?

See what I mean about the black middle class needing the Black Subculture to enrich themselves?

The story also says that her previous job paid from $65,000 to $85,000 —her actual pay is disputed in the PD article—to recruit students for the Cleveland Metropolitan School District.

Why do we need someone to do this? Do they pay people to do this stuff in the suburbs? If you live in Cleveland, you go to the Cleveland public schools. Why do you need to recruit students? Maybe they needed her to bring in some dropouts, I don't know, but the whole thing sounds ludicrous to me.

Tobias added: "In a resume provided to the county, McCoy said she worked between 2006 and 2013 as executive program director for the Community Covenant Oversight Team, a group focused on helping black males in the ninth grade."

Once again this shows how the black middle class needs the BSC to survive. For seven years she was doing the job of the kids' parents. Do you know how many of these type programs there are in Cuyahoga County? More than I can count.

One more time. Why does the BSC generate these kind of jobs? Because the black males have no fathers, that's why.

Here's another personal story to illustrate why the black middle class needs the BSC to exist. And this will explain why they are not going to be voting for any leaders who want to end the BSC's dependence on the government anytime soon.

Early in my career I wrote a book called *League Park*. It was the old baseball field that the Cleveland Indians played in from 1891 until 1947. It was also the home field for a black baseball team called the Cleveland Buckeyes before our national pastime integrated. And it just so happened to be smack dab in the middle of Cleveland's "Hough Neighborhood," the site of the 1966 racial riots.

Of course, it was a white neighborhood when the Indians played there but then the neighborhood flipped. Well, I was young and dumb when I wrote the book in 1978 and I had this crazy idea. The old stadium was crumbling but it was still salvageable. I wanted to bring it back to life.

So I partnered with the city of Cleveland's Landmark Commission to make it a Cleveland landmark. That would give it official historical designation and help save it from the wrecking ball while opening up some tax breaks for any remodeling efforts.

We decided to sponsor a "League Park Day" to draw attention to the field's plight and maybe spur some efforts to save it. Luckily, the sports editor for the *Plain Dealer* liked my idea and gave us a big story about "League Park Day" in the paper.

We envisioned a new refurbished baseball park that would become the home field to a local college team. Lots of young ballplayers would love the opportunity to play on the same grounds as legends like Babe Ruth, Ty Cobb and Tris Speaker. A "Field of Dreams" kind of thing.

We also envisioned turning the old ticket office building, still standing near the corner of the field, into a Cleveland baseball museum, sort of a miniature version of The National Baseball Hall of Fame in Cooperstown, New York.

So we threw a big party. We invited a lot of former major league stars, sold t-shirts and hamburgers, and drew a big crowd. I thought we were on our way to saving the old field. But I did not understand how the black middle class functioned.

At the time the old ticket office was being used by the United Way charity for its office to help the neighborhood youth. The only new part of the old park's grounds was a basketball court.

So we met with the black guy running the "United Way Center" and ran our ideas about saving the old ballpark by him. His reaction? He told us in no uncertain terms that he did not want a bunch of white guys from the suburbs coming into his neighborhood and telling him what to do. That put an end to that idea.

Wow. Besides, I did not appreciate being called a white suburbanite since I was living as far into the west side's inner city as he was on the east side. I could not understand his attitude. I thought it was a no brainer that a new League Park would be an economic engine for the neighborhood.

It wasn't until later that I figured out that he probably felt that his job would have been threatened by our success. He needed all those poor struggling black youths to keep him in business. They were his bread and butter.

If we were correct, the museum would bring in tourists and the playing field would bring in players and fans. The park would hire neighborhood kids as service and maintenance workers bringing in jobs where they were sorely needed. No such luck.

Ironically, the fire station that I would later work at for most of my east side tour was right down the street from League Park. So I eyewitnessed its slow demise. And as I watched League Park self-destruct I noticed some interesting news items in the papers.

Like how in 1990 a Negro Leagues Baseball Museum opened in Kansas City. League Park could have done that with its connection to the Cleveland Buckeyes.

More recently President Obama announced that his Presidential Library was going to be located in the South Side of Chicago where he started his political career as a "community organizer."

The South Side of Chicago is definitely a BSC neighborhood. Yet the Associated Press stated: "The library ... is expected to be a boon to nearby communities that struggle with gang violence, drugs and unemployment. The University of Chicago has said the library and its 800,000 expected visitors a year will translate into dozens of new businesses, thousands of jobs and tens of millions of dollars in revenue."

Of course, I am not comparing League Park to a presidential library. But the United Way Center eventually closed and the old baseball field became a hangout for hoodlums.

Thankfully, old ideas never die. So a few years ago, much to my surprise, I opened my newspaper and discovered that the city of Cleveland was finally going to spend a couple million dollars to renovate old League Park.

It only took about 35 years for the city of Cleveland to pick up on my idea. There was not as much left to save as before but in 2014 the city actually pulled it off. They dedicated the newly refurbished field and ticket house. And it is a beautiful gem in the old Hough neighborhood.

I was so surprised by this that I thought just maybe there is finally hope for our African American brothers and sisters. That we could transition from a dependency-based BSC economy into a job-based Black Prosperous Culture.

I even thought maybe our first African American president, Barack Obama, might lead the way. But then I remembered that he was an

Affirmative Action guy himself. In his six years as our fearless leader, instead of creating real jobs for his people, he has instead added many more government jobs that need even more citizens on our welfare rolls to justify their existence. All the while putting us deeper and deeper in debt. Kind of like the League Park guy.

Let's go to the next chapter and discover why.

CHAPTER FIFTEEN:
BARACK OBAMA,
OUR FIRST AFFIRMATIVE ACTION PRESIDENT

"Since I took office, we cut our deficits by two-thirds ... middle class economics ... That's theory we've tried since I took office and today we have dramatically lower deficits," Barack Obama, in his op-ed piece published in the Plain Dealer *on March 21, 2015, three days after speaking to the Cleveland City Club.*

BEFORE WE DISCUSS President Barack Hussein Obama I hope you were paying attention during the Affirmative Action chapter. Barack Obama has to be the least qualified American to ever sit in the Oval Office of the White House.

Let's just take a second to compare him to his predecessor, George W. Bush, who the media still loves to bash. Bush was governor of Texas, one of the largest and most prosperous states in the union, with a billion-dollar-plus budget. And he was a jet pilot in the Texas Air National Guard. Do you think just anyone can fly a jet airplane? But Bush never received any respect from the media because he was a conservative Christian Republican president.

And it is Great State of Texas that is creating all the jobs that President Obama took credit for in his City Club speech on "middle class economics." Without the Lone Star State all of Obama's stats would have looked pretty pathetic. Thank you, former Republican Texas Governor Bush and his 15-year successor, Republican Governor Rick Perry.

Back to the president. A white guy with Barack Obama's qualifications would have been laughed off the podium by the national media. But because he was a black guy who could talk like a white guy he was given the Democratic Party's nomination because they knew he could bring out the black voters.

Let us take a quick look at his biography. It is pretty typical of the BSC except for one important fact: he had a white mother. In typical BSC fashion his black father barely knew him. He was raised by his white mother and white grandparents in a middle class environment in Hawaii, hardly a disadvantaged neighborhood. If you look at some of his class photos he was practically the only black kid in the classroom. He was even known as "Barry."

If he had been raised by his black father in the BSC instead of his white mother he would have turned into a totally different person with a totally different future. But once he graduated from high school he discovered that he wasn't going anywhere touting the Irish side of his family, even though they were the ones who raised him.

You would think he would go around with a big four-leaf clover on his lapel considering what the Irish side of his family did for him. But instead he became the African American "Barack," and a whole slew of Affirmative Action type opportunities opened up to him.

What ones we may never know because he has refused to make public his high school and college grades. His higher education career occurred while Affirmative Action was all the rage so his grades became a big issue during the 2012 election.

Pundits wondered how a self-proclaimed high school stoner was able to attend Occidental College, an exclusive West Coast school, and then go on to Ivy League colleges like Harvard and Columbia. They figured a white guy with his qualifications probably never would have been admitted. I still haven't seen his grades so we may never know if he took advantage of Affirmative Action or not. My guess is he did.

Don't take me wrong. I actually kind of like Barry. I think he would have been great as a college professor passing on the liberal mantra to another generation of naïve college kids. He can sling the bull with the best of them. His problem is that he believed all that baloney they taught him at Harvard. He has very little experience in the real world.

He spent a few years as a "community organizer," whatever that is, and then went straight into academia. Once again, don't get me wrong. I do not dislike college professors. I am a firm believer in higher education. But you have to take everything you learn there with a grain of salt since they all live in this "ivory tower" insulated from the rest of the country. You have to take all the ideas they embed in your mind and test them out in the real world. See if they can pass the reality test.

Obama never did that. He hid under the cloak of public service and academia. He went straight from academia into politics. He has no business being one of the most powerful men on the planet. He reminds me of the black AA fire chiefs on the Cleveland Fire Department. It was only thanks to AA that they were promoted up the ranks from fireman to Fire Chief of the City of Cleveland.

They had no business being CEOs of a multi-million dollar government department. They were totally unqualified for the position. But once a week they would put on their fancy uniforms and strut their stuff over at Cleveland city hall in front of our black mayor and black city councilmen. It kept their black constituents happy.

The only problem was that under their AA leadership we went from being one of the best fire departments in the country to being a scandal-ridden corrupt city division that was constantly in the newspapers for all the wrong reasons. The same thing is happening to our great country.

It will take decades before we fully understand the damage inflicted on our great nation by Barack Obama. This is especially true of his signature policy, Obamacare. It is like Lyndon Johnson's "Great Society." We are still trying to get ourselves out from under that disaster. Democrats need to learn that more often than not government programs are the heart of the problem, not the solution.

For example, a few years ago we had the greatest health care system in the world. Average citizens and even kings from around the world would come to my town's Cleveland Clinic for world class health care. Uninsured members of the BSC would also be treated there. They just wouldn't pay their bills. The Clinic would have to eat millions of dollars of unpaid expenses every year but that was a part of doing business in a BSC neighborhood. No one was ever turned away.

To understand Obamacare you have to refer back to my "school busing" chapter. It is about giving free health care to the BSC. Obama's plan was to have the working people pay more money for their insurance so they could expand coverage for the BSC segment that does not work and does not have coverage. He did not want to call it a tax but it is one.

Obamacare does the same thing for our medical patients that school busing did for our school children. It screws up the whole medical system for both blacks and whites by giving the federal government a role in it. It created a huge government bureaucracy with so many unintended consequences that no one knows what it is doing. It will take us years to sort out this mess.

In the meantime our once great medical system, a huge part of our economy, is an economic train wreck running off the rails at an alarming speed. But while school busing only cost our school boards millions of dollars to implement, Obamacare is costing America's taxpayers billions of dollars.

I almost had the opportunity to ask him about our debt crisis. On March 18, 2015, I went down to the Cleveland Convention Center to listen to the President of the United States of America, Barack Hussein Obama, give a speech at the city club of Cleveland, a bastion of free speech since 1912. The City Club has been visited by many U.S. presidents during its illustrious history.

The main reason for Obama's talk was to explain his agenda for "middle class economics." His speech was mostly a comparison of his economic theory versus his portrayal of the Republican theory. He said the Republicans are still trying to sell their old "trickle-down theory of economics" which he says only helps the rich, not the middle class.

His speech was a warm-up for a tough upcoming budget battle on Capitol Hill with a brand new Republican Congress. The Republicans gave the Democrats a good whupping in the previous election, taking control of both the House of Representatives and the Senate. The voters had sent the president a strong message about their feelings on his economic policies. So he was travelling the country justifying them during his last two years in office. He was giving speeches that attempted to frame his place in history in his own terms.

I enjoyed his speech. The venue was small and comfortable and I was fortunate to be one of only 475 citizens invited to attend. He was relaxed but serious with some nice humor thrown in for good measure. The crowd was definitely friendly which was very apparent during the question-and-answer period after his speech.

He mostly blew his own horn, casting himself as another FDR. Whereas FDR brought our country back from "The Great Depression" of the 1930s, he brought us back from "The Great Recession" of 2008. He spouted many statistics to back up his claim that because of his actions and those of the Democratic Congress that was voted in with him in 2008, the economy was now booming and Obamacare was a huge success.

I did have a little problem with his sense of history. Mainly because my parents and grandparents lived through the Great Depression of the 1930s and for over a decade they didn't have two nickels to rub together. Huge crowds of Americans stood in long lines just for some free bread to feed their children.

I, on the other hand, experienced the 2008 Recession. Although my house lost some of its value, nothing changed that much for me or any of my working friends. It was nothing like the Depression that lasted a decade after 1929. I know just from comparing stories with my parents that Obama was blowing smoke. But we can discuss the validity of his statistics another day. I want to focus on a couple of small items from his speech.

Obama repeated the same mantra in an op-ed column that he wrote for the March 21, 2015 *Plain Dealer*.

The headline was: MIDDLE CLASS ECONOMICS WORKS FOR ALL AMERICANS.

He wrote:

"Since I took office we cut our deficits by two-thirds."

AND

"middle-class economics ... That's the theory we tried since I took office, and today we have dramatically lower deficits."

We need to discuss President Obama's comments on our federal deficit. He did mention the budget deficit a few times. Both times he bragged that the federal deficit was cut by two-thirds during his watch.

I needed to beg to differ with his terms. I had my hand up during the question-and-answer session but he didn't call on me. Before his speech, Don Moulthrop, Executive Director of the City Club, challenged us to ask tough questions. "The City Club has a tradition of allowing normal citizens to ask tough questions of our leaders," he said. "Take advantage of it."

I thought that was a great viewpoint. It is extremely rare for a normal citizen like myself to have the opportunity to address our country's leader. It is what makes this such a great nation. It was the reason I attended his speech. Like I said, it was a very friendly Democratic crowd.

The audience threw him mostly softballs so he could expand on his biased view of our economy.

I raised my hand but he did not call on me. But here is what I was going to ask him if he had called on me.

"Hello, Mr. President. Welcome to Cleveland. My big concern is our national debt. The last I heard it was approaching 18 trillion dollars and is growing larger every day. I'm worried that my children and grandchildren are going to be saddled with paying off our debts forever. That all their middle class taxes are going to go to paying interest on them. How does your 'middle class economics' address this issue?"

I am still wondering how he would have answered. Maybe he would have gone back to his claim that he cut the federal deficit by two-thirds example. I wish he would have explained that statement better. I am still not sure what he meant.

Maybe he was suggesting that our yearly deficit is declining. The deficit that is a result of our yearly budget. If that is true I would give him credit for it. At least that is something. But maybe it is more like when President Bill Clinton's budget actually had a surplus. Instead of using it to pare down our debt Clinton spent it to create even more new social programs which added to our long term debt.

Throughout Obama's speech he kept repeating, "All you have to do is look at the facts" to prove his economic recovery is real. So let me expand on some other "facts" from my previous chapters.

If you recall, I quoted reporter Kevin G. Hall of the Tribune Washington Bureau who did a nice job of explaining our deficit problems in the *Plain Dealer* on March 9, 2015.

He stated that: "After years of debt that normally amounted to about a third of the nation's total economy, it has spiked to more than 70 percent with no relief in sight."

He added: "The nonpartisan Congressional Budget Office ... sees the debt level approaching 80 percent in 2025 ... Just eight years ago this number was about 35 percent, about the historical average."

Six years ago Obama became our president.

Hall quoted government economists who said that our debt at 75 percent of our Gross Domestic Product is "the new normal." And that: "Debt went from $7.5 trillion in 2009 to $12.6 trillion in 2014" under Obama.

The sad fact is that Hall's story was already out of date when Obama spoke to the Cleveland City Club less than two weeks later. The same day he spoke there was a different story about our national debt woes in the March 18, 2015 Lorain, Ohio, *Morning Journal*.

Here's the headline: FEDERAL DEBT LIMIT COMES BACK INTO FORCE AT $18.1 TRILLION.

WOW! Associated Press reporter Martin Crutsinger explained that: "After a year with no cap on government borrowing, the federal debt limit has come back into force. The new limit—$18.133 trillion to be exact —was announced by the Treasury Department on Tuesday."

He goes on to explain how the debt limit had been suspended by Congress in 2014 so they wouldn't have to vote on increasing it until after the 2014 elections. In other words they didn't want the American people to know how bad things were until after the election.

And even more frightening is that we would probably have gone past the debt limit already, which is illegal, except Treasury Secretary Jacob Lew had to pull some fancy bookkeeping maneuvers to keep the government operating. He borrowed money from some "pension and disability funds for government employees." But he says he will pay them back once Congress approves "a new debt ceiling." In other words, when it increases the debt ceiling again.

Are you kidding me? Does anyone know how crazy this all is? Does the Treasury Secretary ever explain to the president what he has to do to keep our government running? Does Obama get it or does he just choose to ignore it? They might as well just scrap the whole "debt limit" thing anyway. The way things are going our leaders will never be able to get this under control.

Our kids and grandkids are doomed. I am still wishing that Obama had called on me at the Cleveland City Club. After explaining his deficit reduction strategy I would have told him that there is another way to solve our nation's debt dilemma. Pick up a copy of *Why America Is Bankrupt*. Hell, I'd even give him a free copy.

CHAPTER SIXTEEN:
EAST CLEVELAND, DETROIT AND BALTIMORE:
The Future of America?

"A state lawmaker representing East Cleveland is pushing a budget amendment that would give the financially beleaguered city more than $6.7 million in state funding. Rep. Kent Smith, a Euclid Democrat, said he's seeking the money from the state's 'rainy day' fund because East Cleveland has run out of ways to raise revenue and has suffered from law makers' cuts to local government funding."—from the Plain Dealer's *"Newswatch" on April 10, 2015.*

IF YOU WANT to look at the future of America, it is time to take a hard look at three communities: East Cleveland, a suburb of Cleveland that is predominantly black, Detroit, another predominantly black city that was once one of the largest and most prosperous cities in America, and Baltimore, the site of recent racial protests because of the death of a black citizen under police custody.

Let's start with East Cleveland because I know it up close and personal. If you recall from my Cleveland Fire Department chapter I was quite busy fighting fires my first ten years on the job when Cleveland's east side was burning down.

Well, sometimes we would even go over our border and help another community called East Cleveland put out their fires. I never thought much about it. It was part of the excitement of the job.

I remember one time a big old apartment building was on fire and a black East Cleveland fire chief, not a fireman but a chief, saw us pull up on the scene. He came over and asked me what I wanted his men to do. If he knew anything about the Cleveland Fire Department, he would have noticed that I had a blue stripe on my helmet. You wear a blue stripe to let the other firemen know that it is your first year on the job and watch out for you because you are still learning the profession.

But I was young and cocky and I had already seen my share of "working fires" as we called them. So I told him to put a ladder up and help us ventilate the roof which we were going to do.

I should have used this story in the "Affirmative Action" chapter but it applies here because East Cleveland did not have enough firemen to protect its citizens. They were always calling us for assistance.

Fast forward thirty years later. There is a television story about how East Cleveland was having trouble finding the funds to fix one of its fire trucks. And then there was a fire that burned down three homes. I did not hear the specifics but I bet our guys helped them stop the fire from burning down the whole neighborhood.

East Cleveland should be the poster boy for the whole Black Subculture. It is at least ninety percent African American. But it has a great history. Once upon a time it was THE place to move when Cleveland residents wanted to escape the crowded inner city.

John D. Rockefeller, at one time the richest man in the world, owned an estate there. Today his estate is a nice park for the East Cleveland residents. Then the suburb flipped from white to black as I explained in the chapter "There Goes the Neighborhood."

The problem with East Cleveland is the same problem I have been preaching this whole book about the BSC. Since so many of its residents are on welfare, they don't bring in enough taxes. There is not enough money to pay the police and firemen or buy a new garbage truck.

Please reference the quote above by the state representative asking for money from the state of Ohio's "rainy day" fund to help it pay its bills.

First of all, why does Ohio have a "rainy day" fund approaching a billion dollars? Because a Republican Governor, John Kasich, and a Republican legislature turned the state around after the previous Democratic Governor left them with a "rainy day fund" of 89 cents and a projected $8 billion deficit.

However, Rep. Smith blames East Cleveland's problems on cuts from the state to local governments but East Cleveland has needed special help from the state for years, not only to pay its employees but to audit its books and fund its school system.

Here is what many Ohioans do not understand. There is some hard-working farmer in central Ohio who is out in his fields toiling all day in the hot sun to grow the corn and wheat that we need to feed our children. And the state of Ohio is asking him to take some of his tax money and to give it to a community with loads of residents who do not work or pay taxes. There should be a law against this sort of thing.

This is why I say beware of the signs from East Cleveland. If our nation does not dramatically change its ways our whole country may end up just like it, a bankrupt shell of its former self.

There is a plan afoot to save the bankrupt suburb. Some of its residents want the city of Cleveland to annex it. Then all the white suburban taxpayers who work downtown would once again have to foot the bill to save their unfortunate fellow BSC citizens. However, East Cleveland's political leaders are against the idea because they might lose their cushy positions. (See the chapter on the black middle class.)

Of course, most of Cleveland's taxpayers do not like the idea of bailing out East Cleveland either. They have enough headaches of their own without adding to them.

There was an interesting discussion about East Cleveland on a recent local radio talk show that illustrates my point of view.

It went something like this:

A black guy from East Cleveland calls the show to complain about a blinking traffic light by his house that is being used as a trap to write traffic tickets by the police. He also complains about East Cleveland's traffic cameras, saying most of the fines they collect go to the camera company instead of the city.

But as he continues talking with the radio show host about his neighborhood, the guy admits that even though he has paid off his house he feels trapped there. (Just like my "There Goes the Neighborhood" chapter.)

The radio host agrees, saying that he has driven through parts of East Cleveland and it looks like a war zone filled with abandoned houses. (Similar to the east side neighborhoods I worked in as a fireman.)

Then here came the kicker.

The host asks the guy: "You can't sell your house, can you?"

The caller: "You won't believe it but you can buy a house in East Cleveland for $150." (That is one hundred and fifty dollars)

Host: "Oh, I believe it."

Caller: "Those houses used to be worth $30,000. My house was once worth $100,000."

I'm listening to this conversation while I'm driving in my car so I am screaming at the radio. "Yeah, baby, this is exactly what I am talking about, my fine black brother." I am happy that this dude who lives in the hood agrees with my premise that the BSC is killing the tax base.

Now take all the problems in East Cleveland and multiply them by thousands and you have what we used to call our "sister city," Detroit, Michigan. When I was growing up Detroit was one of the largest cities in the country with something over a million and a half residents. The auto industry was booming and America practically owned a monopoly on the production of automobiles.

Cleveland was somewhat of a satellite of Detroit. We had our own collection of auto plants and many manufacturing factories that fed them auto parts. My father worked at a Chevy plant near our house when he was first married. He liked the job but my mother did not like him working the night shift and as usual Mom ruled. Looking back, he should never have left.

The reason he should have stayed at the Chevy plant is because thanks to its strong union, the United Auto Workers (UAW), he was earning a decent salary with an excellent benefits package. He would have enjoyed a prosperous retirement instead of a difficult one.

But the city of Detroit and the entire auto industry fell into bad times and here is why. After President John F. Kennedy (yep, back to the 60s again) was elected he was approached by some of the black leaders who helped him garnish the black vote. They wanted some jobs for their people, a reasonable request.

They came up with an idea that was called "jaw-boning." Even our president does not have the power to force companies to hire people. But Kennedy had a lot of pull with the UAW and he kind of twisted the arms of the auto companies and the union to hire African Americans.

Once it started, of course, the word spread swiftly. Many Southern blacks migrated to Detroit. A similar phenomenon occurred at the two auto plants near my house in Cleveland, one Ford, one Chevy. Many of my friends went straight from high school into the auto plants. And here is what they told me happened.

As I explained in the school busing chapter from my experience, the black kids had a terrible work ethic. But once they were hired the auto industry was stuck with them. You could not fire or discipline them without a pushback from the NAACP.

So quality control at the Ford and Chevy plants suffered. I'll spare you the details of the stories my friends told me. Let it be known that when the white guys saw what the black guys were getting away with, they followed their lead.

And the United Auto Workers union is required to defend their members no matter how incapably they perform their job. (I've seen this similar scenario thanks to Affirmative Action on the fire department.) So the union suffered likewise.

Slowly but surely America's auto plants began putting out a junk product. In the 1970s we called them "rust buckets." That was fine as long as America owned the automobile monopoly and controlled most of the market share. The big three, Ford, Chrysler and General Motors, were flush with so much money there was plenty to go around. But no one saw the competition from the Japanese on the horizon.

It was not long before Toyotas and Hondas were filling our highways as American consumers became fed up with the Big Three's product. It would take decades for the auto industry to recover from President Kennedy's "jaw-boning" tactic.

It was not a pretty sight. Flash forward 35 years again and take a look at the city of Detroit. It flipped just like East Cleveland. Much of Detroit now looks like our radio host described East Cleveland, a war zone.

Now Detroit is the largest city in America to declare bankruptcy. It almost had to sell off the treasurers from its excellent art museum to satisfy its creditors. Police and firemen like myself are struggling to keep their pensions from being slashed.

Is this the future of America? Maybe. Unless we change our ways.

Detroit has had its share of racial riots in the past but it is Baltimore's that are in the news as I write this book. So let's take a quick look at what happened in Baltimore.

Police there arrested a 25-year-old black man named Freddie Gray who died in the back of the police van on his way to jail. His spine was severed during the trip so the black community cried "police brutality" and rioted and looted in response.

It was just one of many such riots in different cities throughout the year for similar claims. In this case, Freddie Gray already had a long rap sheet. But Marilyn Mosby, the state's attorney general, quickly filed criminal charges against the six police officers involved; three of them were even African American. Some columnists argued that she was more interested in calming the riots than dispensing justice.

Be that what it may, we'll let the courts sort out that mess. What I found interesting was an article in the May 15, 2015 *The Week Magazine* by Terrence McCoy that blamed Gray's problems on lead poisoning. According to McCoy, Gray's family won an undisclosed settlement from their landlord because there was paint peeling from the walls in the house Gray grew up in. They claimed young Freddie probably ate some of the paint and it hampered his development.

I don't know how many kids go around eating paint off their floors but lead poisoning is also a cash cow for lawyers in my town of Cleveland, Ohio. But here's the difference between the BSC and my friends and family.

I've already explained to you how my grandmother's house was in the inner city just like Freddie Gray's. And how many of my friends from West Tech High School lived in similar homes. Many of them were renters throughout their childhoods. But the first thing they did when their family moved in was to try to get the landlord to paint the walls. And if he wouldn't do it they would try to get him to at least buy the paint so they could paint it themselves. And if that didn't work they would spend $20, go out and buy a gallon of paint, and do it themselves anyway.

The real question that I would like to know is whether Gray's family's lead poisoning problems stemmed from using Section 8 rent money. Like I explained earlier this is a slum landlord's dream. The government pays the rent every month and does a terrible job of enforcing the building codes. That's why the federal government needs to get out of the housing business.

To understand the BSC attitude we need to look at one of my favorite fire department stories. It was told to me by a fellow lieutenant who was working at the fire station near where I grew up. Remember how I mentioned that I used to walk through one of the largest government housing projects on my way to school every day? That was when the projects were populated with white war widows trying to raise their kids without dads, the reason the government started ADC in the first place.

A few years ago there was a fire in an oven at one of the units in "the projects." Now the projects are inhabited by mostly black people. The firemen put out the fire and after clearing out the smoke discovered that the oven was caked in grease. It was an accident waiting to happen.

So the lieutenant pointed this out to the black female resident as the cause of the oven fire. He suggested that it needed to be cleaned. So how did the black lady respond?

She asked him who she should call to clean it for her. Do you believe it? This is a prime example of why I wish we had body cameras during my fire department career in the BSC hood.

By reason of its proximity to Washington D.C., Baltimore received millions of dollars over the years in federal social welfare programs. But the BSC chased away local businesses just like in Cleveland and other big cities. And what was the result?

According to Scott Novak in the *Baltimore Sun*, today only about 42 percent of the adults in Freddie Gray's neighborhood are employed." That's about 60 percent unemployment. Great job, Democrats. Keep voting for them, my black brothers and sisters.

I like what Larry Elder, an African American commentator, said about the Baltimore subject as quoted in the same May 15, 2015 issue of *The Week*. Here we go:

"Spare me the victimization," said Larry Elder, in *RealClearPolitics.com*. "Baltimore is run by a black mayor, a mostly black city council, and a black police commissioner; 40 percent of its cops are black. Yet liberals keep telling blacks 'of their continuing oppression,' when the real problem is that 70 percent of black children are born to unwed mothers."

Amen to that, my brother.

It is only a matter of time before another police shooting sparks more riots and protests in another American big city. I just hope it isn't mine.

Democrats want to blame the cops for all their failures over the past 50 years. But let me say it one more time so it will sink in. It is the Black Subculture that the Democrats' policies created in the first place that are at the heart of the problem.

Our once great American cities are rotting from the inside out. So what does our current African American Democratic President Barack Obama propose we do to repair all our inner city strife? He wants to create another program titled "My Brother's Keeper" to help our disadvantaged inner city minority black youth. Does this sound familiar or what?

In my town of Cleveland, Ohio, there are so many programs designed to help "disadvantaged inner city youths" that you could write another book explaining all of them. What I'd like to know is what are the price tags for all these programs? What does it cost our taxpayers to subsidize all these BSC cities like Detroit, East Cleveland and Baltimore? Show me the money, honey.

Of course, they do help a kid here and there, and when they do it is highlighted in the media. But overall they are merely putting a bandaid on a cancer that has been spreading throughout our inner city populations for the past 50 years.

It is time to try some new solutions to these half-century-old problems. It is time to kill the cancer at its source, the misguided federal assistance programs that create more problems than they solve.

CHAPTER SEVENTEEN:
ILLEGAL IMMIGRANTS PAY FEW TAXES ALSO

SINCE THIS BOOK is about how the Democrats sold their soul to the Black Subculture (BSC) for their votes and bankrupted our nation while doing it, I could not end my treatise without mentioning their latest scheme. They are trying the same modus operandi to corral the Latino vote.

I can hear my critics crying already. First, you pick on the poor black people, now you are picking on the poor Latinos. Weren't your people immigrants also? Weren't we all?

I already told you my family's story. The first thing they did when they stepped off the boat from the old country was register at Ellis Island. Then they went right to work and started paying taxes for the privilege of being here, just like I did when I turned 16 years old.

Right now there is a controversy going on over President Obama's latest "Immigration Reform" plan which many people call amnesty. He wants to give about a million illegal immigrants Social Security numbers that will make them legal. Why? Because that's another million or so Democrat voters, of course.

The Democrats argue that they will pay even more taxes once they become legal immigrants. But how do they pay taxes if they are here illegally? They file their taxes using an Individual Taxpayer Identification Number (ITIN) instead of a Social Security number. That means they can even qualify for tax refunds.

Conservatives argue that the taxes they pay don't come anywhere close to the billions of dollars that federal, state and local governments spend on undocumented workers. And giving them Social Security numbers will qualify them for even more benefits.

Neither side knows what will happen when and if Obama's amnesty plan plays out. Kind of like Obamacare.

The first question we need to ask ourselves about our illegal immigration problem is how much is it costing us? I do not think anyone really knows. The illegal immigrant culture is similar to the BSC in that both demand a myriad of social services and pay little in taxes. And the problems with both cultures stem from unwed moms using their babies to qualify for lots of free stuff.

In the case of illegal immigrants, an eight month pregnant woman sneaks across the border and drops her baby here. Since our hospitals never turn away anyone, right off the bat we are footing the medical bills for the mom. And since anyone born on American soil is automatically a citizen, the baby becomes an American citizen and the mother becomes the mother of an American citizen which gives her privileges in our welfare system. Their next move is to sneak more relatives across the border who can also feed off the baby's rights. Multiply that scheme by hundreds of thousands of illegals and you can understand why we find ourselves drowning in debt.

Who would invent such a system? Who is responsible for this crap? What the heck are we doing letting them in here in the first place?

Not only are the illegals helping to bankrupt America, they are draining valuable resources from our southern and western states like Texas, Arizona and California. We now have some states that have huge deficits not unlike our federal government.

Let's take a look at California. Back when I was in high school California was so rich that higher education was free there. I had relatives who lived there so I considered moving there for a year to establish residency and take advantage of their free college opportunities.

I didn't do it but a lot of baby boomers did. And guess what? It's not free anymore. California is now billions of dollars in debt and some of its cities like Compton and San Bernardino have recently asked for bankruptcy protection, à la Detroit.

Why? It is a combination of their large BSC and their huge number of illegal immigrants. Any state or city can only give away so much free stuff before it runs out of funds.

Another problem with our illegal immigrants is the quality of our visitors. I was listening to National Public Radio (NPR) on March 10, 2015. You may be surprised that I listen to the left-leaning NPR even though I am a conservative but I am open to all arguments, right, left and center. My car radio buttons cover the whole spectrum of viewpoints.

Anyway, NPR reported that U.S. Immigration officials announced that they had caught over 2000 illegal immigrants with criminal records like rape and gang affiliation who were bragging about their exploits. Some of them were already deported once before but had snuck back into our country again. Do they pay any taxes on the money they make selling drugs or stealing cars? I doubt it.

My main question is how many illegal immigrant criminals are still here? I doubt if anyone has a clue. And how many total illegals do we even have? I've seen estimates from 7 million to 20 million but how do we even know? I think the government is just making up the number as it goes along.

I have worked for the census bureau a couple times when our nation did its ten year counting. And I can tell you one thing I learned about our census bureau. It is an inexact science. It depends on the honesty of our citizens to tell the census takers the truth. And I can tell you from my experience that a lot of our citizens like to fudge the numbers, especially the ones new to our country who are afraid to be counted.

So what are we supposed to do about our illegal brethren? We have to do something before they break the bank. This is going to be a tough nut to crack. How do we ship millions of illegals back over the border even if we knew who they were and where they are? And what about all the criminals among them?

How many of them are terrorists or drug cartel members who like to kill cops, judges and journalists, the backbone of our democratic system, like they do in Mexico? We are going to need desperate measures to protect our nation from its enemies within.

My first plan of action is to put a halt to all immigration for five years until we fix our broken system. Not only those from our southern border but from Europe, Asia and South America as well. Another big source of illegal immigrants is the foreigners who come here on temporary visas and just do not go back when they are supposed to. They just disappear into the countryside. We need to treat them just like the illegals who slip across the southern border.

Why? Because we have too many people living here already. I know, social planners like to say that we need more immigrants to stimulate our economy but they are just blowing smoke. We don't need any more mouths to feed when half our BSC citizens are unemployed.

Our next important action is to finally secure our southern border to stop the flow of illegals. Then we will have to figure out what to do with all the illegals already here. I have ideas on both of these topics but before we go there we must first take the big giant step, the mother of all actions.

As it is now, anyone who is born on our pay dirt is automatically an American citizen. We are going to have to change the ground rules about how to become an American citizen. We will need a constitutional amendment that states that it is no longer enough to be born in the USA to become a citizen. It will also be required that both parents must either be citizens or legal registered immigrants.

Once we have our new amendment in effect we are going to have to really secure our southern border. We should look across the oceans to Saudi Arabia and Australia for some ideas that work.

The Week Magazine, in its February 20, 2015 issue, reported that "Saudi Arabia is now building a 600-mile wall along its border with Iraq" to keep out ISIS and "is strengthening fortifications along its 1,060-mile border with Yemen." So what are we, a bunch of fools? We're not even as smart as the Saudis?

And you've no doubt heard about all the boats coming into Italy with migrants from the Middle East. In the May 8, 2015 issue of The Week, there was a story about "Europe's Migrant Crisis."

It has a lot in common with ours except their illegals travel by boat instead of foot. The Week reported that over 215,000 migrants came by boat to Italy in 2014. That is nothing compared to our millions of illegals but the whole continent of Europe is freaking out over what to do with them.

The Week said: "Last year a network of Libyan militias collaborated with Italian crime syndicates to make an estimated $170 million in people smuggling."

"Sometimes, smugglers put migrants on a boat with no captain, hand them a compass, and tell them to find their own way to Europe."

Since Europeans keep rescuing them it just encourages more illegals to try the voyage while making criminal "people smugglers" rich. Some politicians overseas are saying Europe should do what Australia does. Their aim is to put the human traffickers out of business with some of the world's harshest border policies. We should take note.

The Week again: "There would be absolutely no resettlement of migrants, the Australian government announced. Instead, the migrants would be towed back to the Indonesian ports they'd set off from, or imprisoned in detention centers in remote Papua, New Guinea before being shipped to destinations such as Cambodia."

"On the surface, the policy worked: Since 2013, only 16 migrant boats have attempted the journey to Australia."

We can learn loads from our Aussie brothers.

Here is what I propose we do to secure our borders. We build two barbed wire fences about twenty feet apart along our entire border with Mexico. Then we put barbed wire on the ground between them. It wouldn't cost that much since it is mostly sticks and wire. I realize that some desperate Mexicans might still take a chance and climb over it. But here is where we go postal on them.

We give the border patrol agents orders to shoot anyone going over the fence. Shoot first and ask questions later like in the old West. We are being invaded so it is time to start fighting back. And more importantly we leave the bodies right where they are to be picked over by the buzzards. The word will spread like wildfire that we mean business from now on. Other illegals will see the skeletons and think twice about giving it a try.

I admit it is a harsh policy but it is working for the Aussies. Once we finally secure the border the next order of business is to address all the illegals already here. We give them two options and we publicize the two options so everyone in America is aware of them.

You can turn yourself in and if you prove you are now a valuable member of our nation then maybe we will let you stay. If you want to stay here, you must tell us what you can do for us. Show us you have a sponsor, someone who will stand up for you like an employer or a neighbor or a pastor. And hold the sponsor responsible if they act like criminals in the future.

Once we set up some strict guidelines there must be no wiggle room for copping out. And if you don't cut the mustard you still get a free ride back to where you came from.

The kicker is what happens if you are caught not turning yourself in. Now you have to face the new consequences. From now on we don't give you a free ride back like we do now. We make the punishment begin to fit the crime.

As it is now our border is basically a revolving door. Once we catch illegals we just export them back home, give them a free bus ride. We have drug cartel criminals who are deported numerous times but just keep coming back because that is the worst that we do to them. This crazy system has to end.

It must be frustrating as hell to our cops and border patrol agents who do all the work of tracking them down just to see them keep coming back over and over again. It's kind of like the suspended student from my old high school who showed up again the next day. What's the deterrent to discourage them from committing the same crime over and over again? There isn't one.

Here is what I propose we do with illegal immigrants the first time our authorities catch the ones who did not turn themselves in. Instead of deporting them we give them a three-month jail sentence. We have to build a huge jail because there are possibly thousands of potential prisoners. But we will hopefully only be keeping them there for three months, just to give them a taste of the prison lifestyle, before we deport them.

We put the jail somewhere cold and desolate like North Dakota and keep the niceties to a bare minimum, similar to the Aussies sending their illegals to Cambodia. No television sets or workout gyms like the fancy federal prisons we use today that are an upgrade from the lifestyle in their native countries.

Then after three months we ID them with fingerprints and DNA tests before we export them. And we let them know in no uncertain terms that if we catch them crossing the border illegally a second time they are going to grow old in the same prison they just left.

I am fairly certain that they will think twice about coming back here again. And the ones who like to come here legally and just stay after the visa expires will also think twice about staying illegally in the first place.

I figure it will take about five years to put our new immigration system in place. And once it is up and running then we can talk about opening our borders again.

What do you say? Who wants to give it a try? Maybe we can put this immigration problem behind us once and for all, just like we can the BSC.

Is there any hope of having some Democrats cross party lines and join us in this important endeavor? Can they really forget about sucking up to the Latinos just to buy their votes?

Or are they still going to follow President Obama's lead? He wants to grant a general amnesty, give all the illegals a Social Security number and let them keep bankrupting the system, adding billions more to our national debt, just like the BSC.

Come on, you old Democrats, remember I used to be one of you. Stand up for your country. Do it for the good old USA.

CHAPTER EIGHTEEN:
WHERE DO WE GO FROM HERE?

WE ARE NEAR the end of my book. This is where the author traditionally ties everything together and offers his own solutions to the problems that he outlined earlier.

But I already did that in Chapter Four, my "Solutions" chapter. The rest of the book was used to explain why my solutions would be needed.

I am going to finish with a third section where I list a number of people who predicted that we would eventually find ourselves in this situation.

I call them the "Voices in the Wilderness."

But for now I want to finish this section with these words:

God Bless America.

May it be "The Land of the Free" and "The Home of the Brave" for many future generations to come.

PART THREE:
VOICES IN THE WILDERNESS

I PROMISED IN my "War on Poverty" chapter that at the end of my book I would list the works of some of what I call "Voices in the Wilderness." These are thinkers who predicted years ago that we would find ourselves in this mess.

The first is Daniel Patrick Moynihan of *The Moynihan Report.* He did his study way back in 1965. It is followed by Dr. Paul Ehrlich's book *The Population Bomb* from 1968. Then there is the 1989 movie *Lean on Me* about a school in 1987. That is followed by Harry Figgie Jr.'s *Bankruptcy 1995* that was written in 1992. Finally, I am going to take some author's liberty and include a couple of my own articles written over the years, especially a tongue-in-cheek satire titled: "Why Can't We All Just Be Democrats?" from 2008.

What we all have in common is a great love of our country. We are all worried about its future. And we all recognize many of the same forces at work that we feel will damage its promise of life, liberty and prosperity for all its citizens.

Here we go.

CHAPTER NINETEEN:
THE MOYNIHAN REPORT
by Daniel Patrick Moynihan

EARLIER I PROMISED a much larger chunk of *The Moynihan Report* so here it is. Please remember that Daniel Patrick Moynihan was a Democrat. He was an Assistant Secretary of Labor in Democratic President Lyndon B. Johnson's cabinet.

And more importantly, he wrote this in 1965, over 50 years ago. I cherrypicked the paragraphs but they are presented in the same order that they were printed. You can find a link to the entire *Moynihan Report* on my web site. (www.peterjedick.com)

Also please pay particular attention to his views on the federal government's Aid to Families of Dependent Children (AFDC) or Aid to Dependent Children (ADC) program. As you know by now, that is the government program that I believe started America on the road to bankruptcy.

Read it and weep, my fellow Americans:

The Negro Family: The Case For National Action
Office of Policy Planning and Research, United States Department of Labor, March 1965

The United States is approaching a new crisis in race relations.

The fundamental problem, in which this is most clearly the

case, is that of family structure. The evidence — not final, but powerfully persuasive — is that the Negro family in the urban ghettos is crumbling. A middle class group has managed to save itself, but for vast numbers of the unskilled, poorly educated city working class the fabric of conventional social relationships has all but disintegrated. There are indications that the situation may have been arrested in the past few years, but the general post war trend is unmistakable. So long as this situation persists, the cycle of poverty and disadvantage will continue to repeat itself.

Chapter II. The Negro American Family

At the heart of the deterioration of the fabric of Negro society is the deterioration of the Negro family.

It is the fundamental source of the weakness of the Negro community at the present time.

The role of the family in shaping character and ability is so pervasive as to be easily overlooked. The family is the basic social unit of American life; it is the basic socializing unit. By and large, adult conduct in society is learned as a child.

But there is one truly great discontinuity in family structure in the United States at the present time: that between the white world in general and that of the Negro American.

The white family has achieved a high degree of stability and is maintaining that stability.

By contrast, the family structure of lower class Negroes is highly unstable, and in many urban centers is approaching complete breakdown.

Nearly a Quarter of Urban Negro Marriages are Dissolved.

Nearly a quarter of Negro women living in cities who have ever married are divorced, separated, or are living apart from their husbands.

Nearly One-Quarter of Negro Births are now Illegitimate.
Both white and Negro illegitimacy rates have been increasing, although from dramatically different bases. The white rate was 2 percent in 1940; it was 3.07 percent in 1963. In that period, the Negro rate went from 16.8 percent to 23.6 percent.

Almost One-Fourth of Negro Families are Headed by Females
As a direct result of this high rate of divorce, separation, and desertion, a very large percent of Negro families are headed by females. While the percentage of such families among whites has been dropping since 1940, it has been rising among Negroes.

The percent of nonwhite families headed by a female is more than double the percent for whites. Fatherless nonwhite families increased by a sixth between 1950 and 1960, but held constant for white families.

It has been estimated that only a minority of Negro children reach the age of 18 having lived all their lives with both of their parents.

Once again, this measure of family disorganization is found to be diminishing among white families and increasing among Negro families.

The Breakdown of the Negro Family Has Led to a Startling Increase in Welfare Dependency.
The majority of Negro children receive public assistance under the AFDC program at one point or another in their childhood.

At present, 14 percent of Negro children are receiving AFDC assistance, as against 2 percent of white children. Eight percent of white children receive such assistance at some time, as against 56 percent of nonwhites, according to an extrapolation based on HEW data.

Again, the situation may be said to be worsening. The AFDC program, deriving from the long established Mothers' Aid programs, was established in 1935 principally to care for widows and orphans, although the legislation covered all children in homes deprived of parental support because one or both of their parents are absent or incapacitated.

In the beginning, the number of AFDC families in which the father was absent because of desertion was less than a third of the total. Today it is two thirds. HEW estimates "that between two thirds and three fourths of the 50 percent increase from 1948 to 1955 in the number of absent father families receiving ADC may be explained by an increase in broken homes in the population."

A 1960 study of Aid to Dependent Children in Cook County, Ill. stated: "The 'typical' ADC mother in Cook County was married and had children by her husband, who deserted; his whereabouts are unknown, and he does not contribute to the support of his children. She is not free to remarry and has had an illegitimate child since her husband left. (Almost 90 percent of the ADC families are Negro.)"

The steady expansion of this welfare program, as of public assistance programs in general, can be taken as a measure of the steady disintegration of the Negro family structure over the past generation in the United States.

Chapter III. The Roots of the Problem

As with the population as a whole, there is much evidence that children are being born most rapidly in those Negro families with the least financial resources. This is an ancient pattern, but because the needs of children are greater today it is very possible that the education and opportunity gap between the offspring of these families and those of stable middle-class unions is not closing, but is growing wider.

Low education levels in turn produce low income levels, which deprive children of many opportunities, and so the cycle repeats itself.

Chapter IV. The Tangle of Pathology
Delinquency and Crime

The combined impact of poverty, failure, and isolation among Negro youth has had the predictable outcome in a disastrous delinquency and crime rate.

It is probable that at present, a majority of the crimes against the person, such as rape, murder, and aggravated assault are committed by Negroes. There is, of course, no absolute evidence; inference can only be made from arrest and prison population statistics. The data that follow [chart not reproduced] unquestionably are biased against Negroes, who are arraigned much more casually than are whites, but it may be doubted that the bias is great enough to affect the general proportions.

Again on the urban frontier the ratio is worse: 3 out of every 5 arrests for these crimes were of Negroes.

In Chicago in 1963, three-quarters of the persons arrested for such crimes were Negro; in Detroit, the same proportions held.

In 1960, 37 percent of all persons in Federal and State prisons were Negro. In that year, 56 percent of the homicide and 57 percent of the assault offenders committed to State institutions were Negro.

The overwhelming number of offenses committed by Negroes are directed toward other Negroes: the cost of crime to the Negro community is a combination of that to the criminal and to the victim.

The Armed Forces

The ultimate mark of inadequate preparation for life is the failure rate on the Armed Forces mental test. The Armed Forces Qualification Test is not quite a mental test, nor yet an education test. It is a test of ability to perform at an acceptable level of competence. It roughly measures ability that ought to be found in an average 7th or 8th grade student. A grown young man who cannot pass this test is in trouble.

Fifty six percent of Negroes fail it.

This is a rate almost four times that of the whites

Alienation

The term alienation may by now have been used in too many ways to retain a clear meaning, but it will serve to sum up the equally numerous ways in which large numbers of Negro youth appear to be withdrawing from American society.

One startling way in which this occurs is that the men are just not there when the Census enumerator comes around.

Along with the diminution of white middle class contacts for a large percentage of Negroes, observers report that the Negro churches have all but lost contact with men in the Northern cities as well. This may be a normal condition of urban life, but it is probably a changed condition for the Negro American and cannot be a socially desirable development.

The only religious movement that appears to have enlisted a considerable number of lower class Negro males in Northern cities of late is that of the Black Muslims: a movement based on total rejection of white society, even though it emulates whites more.

In a word: the tangle of pathology is tightening.

Chapter V. The Case for National Action

The object of this study has been to define a problem, rather than propose solutions to it.

However, the argument of this paper does lead to one central conclusion: Whatever the specific elements of a national effort designed to resolve this problem, those elements must be co-ordinated in terms of one general strategy.

In a word, a national effort towards the problems of Negro Americans must be directed towards the question of family structure. The object should be to strengthen the Negro family so as to enable it to raise and support its members as do other families. After that, how this group of Americans chooses to run its affairs, take advantage of its opportunities, or fail to do so, is none of the nation's business.

The fundamental importance and urgency of restoring the Negro American Family structure has been evident for some time. E. Franklin Frazier put it most succinctly in 1950:

"As the result of family disorganization a large proportion of Negro children and youth have not undergone the socialization which only the family can provide. The disorganized families have failed to provide for their emotional needs and have not provided the discipline and habits which are necessary for personality development. Because the disorganized family has failed in its function as a socializing agency, it has handicapped the children in their relations to the institutions in the community. Moreover, family disorganization has been partially responsible for a large amount of juvenile delinquency and adult crime among Negroes.

Since the widespread family disorganization among Negroes has resulted from the failure of the father to play the role in family life required by American society, the mitigation of this problem must await those changes in the Negro and American society which will enable the Negro father to play the role required of him."

Nothing was done in response to Frazier's argument. Matters were left to take care of themselves, and as matters will, grew worse not better. The problem is now more serious, the obstacles greater. There is, however, a profound change for the better in one respect. The President has committed the nation to an all out effort to eliminate poverty wherever it exists, among whites or Negroes, and a militant, organized, and responsible Negro movement exists to join in that effort.

Such a national effort could be stated thus:

The policy of the United States is to bring the Negro American to full and equal sharing in the responsibilities and rewards of citizenship. To this end, the programs of the Federal government bearing on this objective shall be designed to have the effect, directly or indirectly, of enhancing the stability and resources of the Negro American family.

That is the final statement in *The Moynihan Report* of 1965.

Hallelujah, praise the Lord. I couldn't have said it better myself.

I do not understand why liberals were so upset with him when his final conclusion is **to bring the Negro American to full and equal sharing in the responsibilities and rewards of citizenship.**

So what happened? President Johnson declared a "War on Poverty," championed nuclear Negro families and everyone lived happily ever after? Oh, how I wish it were true.

CHAPTER TWENTY:
THE POPULATION BOMB 1968

"The battle to feed all of humanity is over. In the 1970s hundreds of millions of people will starve to death in spite of any crash programs embarked upon now. At this late date nothing can prevent a substantial increase in the world death rate..." Dr. Paul Ehrlich, The Population Bomb. *The opening sentences to his 1968 book.*

DR. EHRLICH'S ARGUMENT back in 1968 was simple. There were too many people in the world and our population was growing too fast to feed us all. He also said it was up to the United States to take the lead in population control because we consumed many more natural resources than the rest of the world.

His book was a hot topic when I was in college in the late 1960s and early 1970s. Why not? He was talking about our generation maybe starving to death.

Of course, his book is now considered alarmist. He didn't understand how inventive American scientists and farmers were. Amazingly, we have raised our food production to keep up with our growing populations. And his book is credited with helping to start our nation's environmental movement.

But I believe Dr. Ehrlich's population predictions were right on the money. When he wrote his book in 1968 we had about 3.5 billion people on our planet. Today we about doubled that with 7 billion mouths to feed.

We can't keep adding more people like we are. Eventually something has to give and when it does it will be ugly.

I remember when I was a child and we visited an uncle in the county next to Cleveland's. My siblings and I would sit in the back seat and see who could count the most cows. Today his small town is a trendy suburb of Cleveland, filled with homes and malls. I'm sure the same thing has happened across our great nation as our urban landscapes expanded. Eventually all these cities will grow into each other and there will be no farmland left in between them to feed us.

There are huge metropolises around the world where people live on top of each other like ants. In India there are 1.2 billion citizens and many of them do not have a toilet to poop in. We are so fortunate to live in this land of plenty we call The United States of America.

Back when I was in college Ehrlich's book did affect my baby boomer generation. All of us college students were taught about it in our sociology classes. We were lectured that we should not have more than two children. Otherwise we were putting our planet in dire straits and the terrible consequences would be our fault.

This was called having an environmental conscience. Kind of like recycling your aluminum cans. And when I look back I realize that most of my college friends and acquaintances followed their advice and only had one or two children.

Meanwhile our nation's black leaders were telling their people to go forth and multiply, don't worry about how to pay for raising them. (Thank you, ADC.) The larger the black minority, the more clout it would have at the voting booth.

So that's how we ended up with the Black Subculture of our inner cities and a nation that will be a minority majority in the near future.

Dr. Paul Ehrlich's book is still an interesting read. Let's hope his predictions will continue to be wrong. But his thesis is another strong argument for ending the welfare programs subsidizing unwed mothers and halting immigration for at least five years in our own country.

Where is the climate change crowd on this issue? They should all be in agreement with me. Americans are the great users of natural resources, they argue. So if humans are upsetting the climate in dangerous ways, what do you think the carbon footprint of 320 million of us are? Wouldn't less people be more environmentally friendly?

Let's make sure we can feed the people we already have here before we add to all our problems. Like Dr. Ehrlich argued in 1968, the world needs a strong America to lead us out of this mess.

CHAPTER TWENTY-ONE:
THE MOVIE *LEAN ON ME* 1989

I REFERENCED THIS movie earlier in my chapter on "West Tech and School Busing." Director John Avildsen of *Rocky* fame and screenwriter Michael Schiffer combined to create a blueprint for saving our inner city high schools. In the process they exposed the struggles facing our African American communities.

They based their movie on the real life career of Joe Clark, the black principal of Paterson, New Jersey's East High, played by Morgan Freeman. What our nation's inner city schools need is a whole army of Joe Clarks. That is how the great C. C. Tuck ran my high school, West Tech, for decades. He used an iron hand. And it worked.

Today our teachers and principals are handcuffed by the U.S. Department of Education. We need to put that entity out of existence and let the school principals run their own schools without federal interference. I once heard a college president speak in a similar vein. He said he knows how to educate college students, he'd been doing it all his life. If the federal government would just let him do his job, college education would be much better and a lot cheaper.

Rent the movie *Lean on Me*. You will be amazed. But prepare to be shocked. It explores the Black Subculture without any blinders on.

CHAPTER TWENTY-TWO:
BANKRUPTCY 1995
by Harry Figgie Jr. 1992

"In 1995, the United States of America, as we know it today, will cease to exist. That year, the country will have spent itself into a bankruptcy from which there will be no return."—Harry Figgie, 1992

I KNEW HARRY Figgie Jr. He sounds like an alarmist like Dr. Ehrlich but he is not. When I discovered that he wrote his book forty years after I knew him it was one of those "ah, ha" moments. It helped convince me that I was fated to write my own book on a very similar subject.

Both Harry and I were big time baseball fans. We both believed that we might play in the major leagues someday. He confessed in his book that one of the reasons he entered Dartmouth College in 1941 was because his father believed that Jeff Tesreau, Dartmouth's baseball coach, was the best college pitching coach in the country.

I was a walk on to Kent State University's freshman baseball team in the spring of 1968. But I was good enough to play shortstop and bat fourth in the lineup. That summer I joined a bunch of my friends back home to play in a Lakewood Class A summer league. There were still enough of us baby boomer hardball players to support those types of leagues in Cleveland and Lakewood, one of its suburbs.

Our team was sponsored by a company called "Automatic Sprinklers." It was one of the many companies owned by Harry Figgie Jr.'s "Figgie International Inc.," a Fortune 500 company with headquarters in Cleveland. You may have heard about a couple of his other companies, Rawlings Sporting Goods and American LaFrance Fire Engines.

I didn't talk to him much that summer. He was like the owner/ general manager. Looking back now I wish I had picked his brain a bit. But he put together an awesome team so his son, Harry Figgie III, could play with us. I believe we would have given Kent's varsity team a run for their money, and that one had two future major leaguers on it, Thurman Munson and Steve Stone.

So how did I discover Harry Figgie Jr.'s book, *Bankruptcy 1995*? When I was writing this book there was a charity event that was receiving a lot of air play on one of our local radio stations. And one of the event's biggest sponsors was "The Figgie Foundation."

It made me wonder if old Harry Figgie was still alive so I looked him up on the Internet and found his obituary. And lo and behold it mentioned his book. So I had to buy a copy.

What an amazing piece of work. It should be required reading for every college economics and political science major in the country. Ditto for all our journalism and history majors.

The only problem is that reading it will scare the hell out of you. In 1992 he predicted a national disaster for our nation in 1995. He figured that in three years the interest on our national debt would become the largest item in our federal budget. And then all hell would break lose.

I believe one of the reasons that his prediction did not come to pass is because in the 1990s we had the computer revolution. Silicon Valley created a whole new industry that pumped jobs and wealth into our national economy. (President Bill Clinton also rode this wave of prosperity even though he had nothing to do with it.)

For instance, when Figgie wrote his book our national debt was at $4 trillion or $16,000 for each man, woman and child in America. And like myself, he blamed President Lyndon Johnson for putting us on the path to destruction.

But then he blasted all the presidents and congressmen from both parties who followed Johnson and never addressed the issue. He predicted our nation would reach a staggering debt of 13 trillion dollars by the year 2000 if nothing was done to stop its growth. I wonder what he would say if he saw our $18 trillion debt today?

It is very interesting how he came upon the subject. He had a reputation as a "cost reduction specialist." So President Ronald Reagan chose him to be co-chairman of his "Private Sector Survey on Cost Control," otherwise known as the Grace Commission.

Figgie learned a great deal about how our government worked while working on the Grace Commission. The Grace Commission submitted a report to President Reagan in January, 1984, with 2,487 cost-saving recommendations. Tragically, very few of them were ever enacted even though many of them would still work today.

It made me wonder if President Obama ever even considered government "cost reduction" during his two terms in office? Figgie realized our country was in desperate shape and by 1992 the numbers scared him so much it inspired him to write his book in hopes of staving off a national disaster.

The Republican United States Senator from New Hampshire, Warren B. Rudman, wrote the "Foreward" to Figgie's book. He co-authored the Gramm-Rudman-Hollings balanced budget law in 1985.

Sadly, he said his bill was mostly "stonewalled" and after 12 years of fighting for debt-reduction chose not to seek re-election.

Here's what Rudman says about Figgie's book, *Bankruptcy 1995.* Remember this is back in 1992:

"Our nation's wealth is being drained drop by drop, because our government continues to mount record deficits and, in order to finance its obligations, puts us at the mercy of foreign lenders.

The security of our country depends on the fiscal integrity of our government, and we're throwing it away."

And more:

"The book you are holding is a godsend. Because it does what the government should have been doing all along. It deals with the issue in a brutally honest, straightforward manner."

And finally:

"We are simply mortgaging the future for the present. And we-and our children and grandchildren-will all pay dearly ... Officials know what needs to be done to cut the growing mountain of debt, and have the talent to do it. But as politicians they lack the will."

"Nothing is more important to the future of our country than getting this problem under control."

Please read Harry Figgie Jr.'s book, *Bankruptcy 1995*. For as Figgie himself said:

"The time to launch an all-out war on deficits was yesterday, but today will have to do."

CHAPTER TWENTY-THREE:
"WHY CAN'T WE ALL JUST BE DEMOCRATS?"

—Peter Jedick, 2008

I REALIZE THAT I do not deserve to be in such acclaimed company as Daniel Patrick Moynihan, Dr. Paul Ehrlich or Harry Figgie Jr. Or even Morgan Freeman. But since I am writing this book I am giving myself a field promotion. We are all soldiers in the war against our national debt crisis.

The main difference between myself and the previous scholars is that while they tried to scare our country into action with predictions of doom, I believe that with the right leadership we can quickly pull ourselves out of this culture of quicksand that we find ourselves in.

Let's look at some of my work that I believe qualifies for the "Voices in the Wilderness" category. You can read them in their entirety in Part Four of this book.

Back in 1982 I wrote a cover story for the Cleveland *Plain Dealer Sunday Magazine* about my experiences as a substitute teacher. At the time I was substituting full time. The way it worked is that early in the morning you would get a call from the school system asking you if you wanted to sub at such and such a school.

Since I wanted to stay busy I was working for three school systems simultaneously: Cleveland, Lakewood and Berea. Lakewood and Berea are a couple of what they now call "inner ring suburbs," i.e. their boundaries touch Cleveland's.

Whoever called first was the school that I would sub for that day.

At the time, the Cleveland schools were starting to feel the disastrous effects of the forced school busing experiment. I experienced up close and personal how the Cleveland schools were dying while the two suburban districts were still flourishing.

Since I was also freelance writing on the side I thought I would write about my experiences. I hoped that once the citizens of Cleveland learned what was going on in their schools they would rise up and put an end to the school busing experiment that was not only destroying the educational opportunities for Cleveland school children but also driving tax paying citizens and businesses out of the city limits.

Wrong. Big wrong. I discovered that way too many people were making way too much money on the school busing experiment. Everyone from bus drivers to lawyers and politicians.

Besides, the media was portraying anyone who was against busing as a "stupid racist hillbilly KKK card carrying nut job." So most people kept their mouth shut and forty years later we still have a Cleveland public school system that is failing miserably at educating its children.

Here's my advice. Rent *Lean on Me* and then read my sub story. The similarities should interest you.

This leads into my second story: "Saying Farewell to West Tech." It was published as an op-ed piece in the *Plain Dealer* in 1995.

I was substituting at my alma mater, West Tech High School, the day it closed. I lamented the fact that they could close a school that was once considered one of the best in the country. I pointed out how out of 1000 students who started there a few years earlier only about 100 were graduating. And how daily attendance was around 50 percent compared to the high 90's when I went there. (Thank you, school busing.)

So I suggested that we needed to break the Cleveland Public School System into six districts like we had six police and fire districts. That would take the federal courts out of the public education business and maybe save the Cleveland schools before it was too late.

Looking back I can see the roots of this book in that article. I wrote about how Germany and Japan studied West Tech after World War II to jump start their war torn countries. Then I added this:

"They learned West Tech's lessons well. Germany's and Japan's economies flourished. Meanwhile our federal government dismantled West Tech while plunging our country into a trillion dollar debt."

I forgot that I even wrote that. But I expanded on the same idea with another op-ed *Plain Dealer* piece the following year. The city of Cleveland's Bicentennial year was 1996. So I wrote a story titled: "Cleveland: Back Up and Start Over."

As a city employee I saw up close and personal how the 200 year old city of Cleveland needed to be redesigned. It was pretty much a corrupt failure at providing government services to its citizens.

So I proposed breaking up the city into six suburbs. From what I could see the suburbs still worked while the city of Cleveland did not, especially in the aforementioned field of education. Smaller governments would be less corrupt and more responsive to their citizens. That in turn would improve police relations. (See today's racial riots in many of our big cities.)

Plus the Cleveland public school system would be eliminated. In one quick move our citizens would change from disgruntled urbanites to happy suburbanites.

This article also contained some ideas that spawned in this book. For example:

"It's time for the city of Cleveland to admit to itself that the urban problems of modern America are just too big to solve."

"Despite massive influxes of federal dollars over the past few decades the neighborhoods have deteriorated, not improved."

Once again my ideas were met with a big yawn. Too many government employees were hauling in big bucks from Cleveland's taxpayers to upset the apple cart. If we had acted quickly we could have stabilized the city's good neighborhoods and targeted the ones that needed assistance. Instead for the past twenty years I've watched the domino effect as urban blight spread. Today so many of Cleveland's neighborhoods have fallen into disrepair that its citizens are among the poorest in the nation.

I had a few other ideas from that story that could be considered for the "Wilderness Voice" category. I also called for a "major overhaul" in our Cuyahoga County government. I said it reminded me of a South American military junta because it was ruled by three county commissioners with a budget of $750 million.

No one knew it at the time but our county government was in for a big upheaval. Many of its leaders would eventually go to jail on corruption charges for playing games with that very budget. The one thing they had in common was that they were all Democrats.

In 2008, before the scandal broke, I wrote my own story about our corrupt county government. I was ahead of the curve again. I was working as a Cuyahoga County poll worker for the election board. It was the primary election that featured presidential candidates Barack Obama and Hillary Clinton.

As a Republican I noticed that my vote was pretty much useless for all the local offices since I lived in Cuyahoga County where all the elected officials were always Democrats.

So I wrote a tongue-in-cheek satire titled: "Why Can't We All Just Be Democrats?" I submitted it to the three main news sources in Cuyahoga County: our daily newspaper, the *Plain Dealer*, our weekly alternative newspaper, the *Free Times*, and our monthly magazine, *Cleveland Magazine*.

Since I was a veteran local freelance writer I had a pretty good relationship with all the editors. I expected at least one of them to publish it. Wrong again. I guess it was a bit too radical for them. For one thing, I compared our one party county government to the Communist party during our cold war with the Soviet Union.

I pointed out that before you could be elected to a government office in Cuyahoga County you first needed the blessing of the Democratic Party. And I added that it helped greatly if you had an Irish surname.

I guess they couldn't take a joke.

I even suggested that all of us Republicans might as well vote in the Democratic primary so we could at least have some say in who was going to be elected. I was talking about local candidates but many Republicans actually did that to have some say about who would be the Democratic presidential candidate, Obama or Hillary.

I eventually did find a news source to publish my story. A new local electronic newspaper called *CoolCleveland.com* published it. The story made its top five list for comment feedbacks.

As I look back on these articles I can see how the seeds for this book were planted in my brain. Maybe someday *Why America Is Bankrupt* will be considered as another "Voice In The Wilderness."

I just hope that this time someone listens.

PART FOUR:
AUTHOR PETER JEDICK'S
PUBLISHED ARTICLES

CHAPTER TWENTY-FOUR:
"OUT OF SCHOOL, Those Who Sub, Babysit"

—from the November 14, 1982 Cleveland *Plain Dealer Sunday Magazine*

Free-lance writer Peter Jedick has been a substitute teacher in the Cleveland Public School system for the past two years. In that time he has taught in all the junior and senior high schools on the city's West Side.

I WAS SUBSTITUTE teaching at West Tech, my old alma mater, and was hoping the experience would be beautiful and nostalgic. Instead it became a disaster when I tried to stop a student for walking out of the homeroom five minutes after the period began.

We scuffled. He dropped a doughnut and in anger I stepped on it and kicked it under a locker. The student returned to the classroom, picked up an iron bar and began beating on desks and radiators. He told other students he would bust my head if I did not pay him 30 cents for the doughnut, which did not belong in the classroom in the first place.

I tried to ignore him.

"Put down the bar and there won't be any problem."

He walked out of the classroom again and I went after him. He returned as the bell rang, iron bar still in his grasp. The other students left and the door locked behind them. No one could enter.

We stared each other down in the quiet of the empty classroom.

"Put the bar down or you're going to find yourself in trouble."

Students gathered outside the glass door. "Hit him, hit him," they chanted.

"If you know my name, you know I'm crazy enough to do this." There was hatred in his eyes.

The tension grew.

Then a security guard came walking down the hallway and the students outside the door hollered out a warning. The student threw the iron bar in a trash can and ran out the door.

Of course, such incidents are not commonplace. But in the last six months of the 1981-2 school year, I had one student take a swing at me, another attack me with his belt, and a class stuff my sweater in a trash bin and spit on it when I stepped out of the room.

I also took a switchblade away from a junior high school girl and heard enough verbal threats to last a lifetime.

As a substitute, I expect to see the unruly side of classroom behavior, but this is ridiculous—and most teachers can rattle off lists of such incidents. It is impossible for them to teach properly under these conditions.

When I was in school, only 15 years ago, a substitute teacher was a rare treat, a break from the routine. Today in Cleveland, I have found it is not unusual for a student to have at least one, and maybe two or three subs a day.

Why?

"The teachers are literally burning out," a music instructor at Lincoln Junior High told me.

They are burning out because teacher welfare has become a low priority in the Cleveland school system. Education is no longer the primary concern of the schools. There is no time for it.

Today's teachers must first deal with discipline, security, theft, vandalism and desegregation—busing.

It wasn't always that way. In 1972-73 I substituted in the Lakewood and Berea systems and remember only one class giving me a major disciplinary problem. I never had to call the office or a security guard for assistance.

Today that "worst class of the year" could be any class in the Cleveland system. But do you blame the new generation of students or the Cleveland system? I substituted again in Lakewood to find out, and the answer is obvious.

You blame the system. Not the entire system, of course. There are exceptions: John Marshall High and Joseph Gallagher Junior High would be considered fine schools in any community.

But most of the schools are choking in a cloud of apathy and despair. Cleveland's teachers were forced to stand idly by as millions of dollars were bestowed on lawyers, consultants, buses and security systems.

Meanwhile they teach in deteriorating classrooms without adequate supplies, pay raises or a sense of security. It has left them bitter and cynical.

The gap I found between the Cleveland and Lakewood systems is so great it cannot be defended with cries of poverty, discrimination or a new generation. The differences lie in such areas as student's work habits, responsibility and respect for teachers.

In Cleveland, a substitute teacher passes out meaningless work sheets or tests. Most of the class does not even attempt to do the assignment. As soon as students discover there is a substitute they either cut out (high school) or invite their friends to visit (junior high). The students are well rehearsed at conning the sub.

In Lakewood, a substitute actually can teach. I take over the class, answer questions, work with the students, do all the things subs did in the past when it was a training ground for new teachers. Education does not skip a beat.

In a typical Lakewood class only one or two students are missing and they are actually absent. If I substitute a shop or science class, the students work on their projects as if their regular teacher were there.

Certain students are responsible for passing out equipment, collecting it and cleaning up.

In Cleveland, shops and labs are always off-limits to subs. "Too many tools were missing each time we had a sub," a John Marshall teacher explained. Like most teachers, he preferred not to be identified.

Teaching in Lakewood is fun. Teaching in Cleveland is a headache.

In Cleveland, depression sets in almost as soon as the teacher enters the building. By the end of the school year many Cleveland buildings resemble the inside of a New York subway. Holes are kicked in walls, glass doors are shattered, graffiti is everywhere, restrooms are closed for repairs and lockers are in shambles. Most classrooms are barren. Even chalk and blackboard erasers are in short supply. Equipment is kept under lock and key.

Lakewood's three junior highs are older than most in Cleveland. Yet I taught in clean, even carpeted classrooms with energy-efficient windows and pleasant hallways. Televisions sets, computers, lab equipment and other teaching aids are scattered around the classrooms for ready use.

"People like to blame Paul Briggs (former superintendent of the Cleveland Schools) for the condition of these new buildings," a maintenance worker told me. "But the problem is vandalism. The same architects built in Parma and Berea and they are in great shape today."

Junior highs everywhere present the greatest challenge to a teacher. In Cleveland, however, a junior high assignment is like contracting herpes. It may not kill you, but you wish someone else had it.

Despite the millions of dollars spent on integration, the typical junior high class I find in Cleveland is composed almost entirely of black students. If there are two or three white students they usually sit together in a corner and do not participate, much like blacks in the pre-civil rights era.

About half the kids do not bring paper, pencils or books to class. Yet there are usually is at least one radio, a few packs of playing cards, a Rubik's cube and a good supply of candy, gum and potato chips.

Many students wear their jackets to class for a quick getaway between periods. And there is almost always a group of students roaming the corridors and hanging around the outside of the buildings.

The high school classes, except at Lincoln West, are better prepared, better behaved and slightly more integrated.

"You should see the students when they come here in the 10th grade," a Marshall science teacher told me. "It takes half the year to teach them to behave."

Meanwhile, in Lakewood, almost every junior and senior high school student brings paper, books and an assortment of pens and pencils to class. No food, no cards, no radios and few jackets. The halls are empty between classes and, except for Lakewood High, there are few students outside the building.

The typical Cleveland class has one other ingredient lacking in Lake-wood and it accounts for many of the differences between the two systems—the adult posing as a junior or senior high school student.

"We have a lot of 19-year olds in the 10th grade," a West Tech assist-ant principal explained. "These kids know they can collect Social Security as dependents until they are 22, so they come to school just long enough for the welfare department to check up on them, then withdraw. Next fall they'll be back."

"It used to be that if a student wasn't achieving and over-age we could force him to go to night school," he said. "Maybe he'd benefit from the adult environment. But today everyone must pay for night school, the state will no longer subsidize a student's night school fees. And the state says everyone has the right to a free education until they're 21."

At Thomas Jefferson Junior High I passed out reports cards. A quarter of the homeroom, 8 of 32 students failed every subject. They are the chronic absentees.

These are the students destroying the educational process and the system's statistics. They show up just often enough to distract the students who do want an education.

Last year, Cleveland's new school board brought in local pro athletes to stimulate student attendance. "Stay away, let 'em go," a junior high teacher laughed when he heard about the program. This is the attitude of most Cleveland teachers. They hope the problem students will leave so they can work with the ones who want to learn.

In Cleveland, the textbooks, new and old, are battered beyond belief, from being thrown as often as carried. Few are allowed to leave the classroom. The school libraries seem relics from a previous civilization.

At Horace Mann Middle School in Lakewood, the librarian complained that students take out only 50-100 books a day. In Cleveland, I subbed for the librarian at Clara Westropp Junior High. Less than a dozen kids visited the library all day, most of those to play cards and watch television. The students checked out three books.

"Kids don't read like they used to," West Tech's librarian said. "Hardly any books are out for research and almost none for pleasure."

Since the students do not read they have trouble writing.

When a fellow substitute and former English teacher said, "Every year we graduate another generation of illiterates," I decided to test her observation, and surveyed the work turned in to me by the students.

The sad fact is that 6th-graders in Lakewood can spell and write better than many of Cleveland's high school seniors, many of whom cannot write a complete sentence.

High school teachers blame the junior highs. The junior highs blame the grade schools. They all blame the great amount of time which must be spent on discipline instead of education.

"The newspapers criticize us for not motivating the students," a West Tech English teacher said. "But motivation cannot be turned on with a switch. It must be taught in the home."

One school which epitomizes the deterioration of the Cleveland Public School system is West Tech, once one of the finest schools in the country. Thanks to the dedicated faculty, it is still one of the friendliest schools in the system. Substitutes hope for an assignment there. But many current and former teachers lament the school's decline.

West Tech opened in 1912 to provide immigrant children with the opportunity to learn a skilled trade as well as absorb American culture and language. As a pioneer technical school it was often visited by educators from across the country and around the world.

It was a magnet school before they were called magnet schools. Any student from Cleveland's West Side who qualified could attend West Tech rather than a neighborhood school. (East Tech provided a similar service on the East Side.)

When I graduated in 1967, West Tech was the largest school in Ohio. Like many other students, I voluntarily took two buses to attend it. It was a school with a reputation for strict discipline and good basic education. Students do not seem to mind the discipline; many of them even attended illegally after the planned construction of I-90 forced their families to move to the suburbs.

Parents loved sending their children to West Tech. There was a list of students waiting to attend. Employers were eager to hire West Tech graduates.

"If you make it the next four years you are practically guaranteed a job the day after graduation," a guidance counselor told us at our freshman assembly. (West Tech was the only West Side high school with its own 9th grade.)

Students chose a major field of study from a long list of skills which included art, business, electronics, home economics, music, foundry, woodworking and welding. Although most students used a chemistry major as a steppingstone to higher education, anyone could combine their technical programs with college preparatory courses. A friend of mine who majored in machine shop, for example, graduated from Kent State University with a sociology degree.

One teacher took a survey during those years and discovered that 30% of the graduates at least started college. "I don't know if they finished or not," he said, "but that's pretty good for a technical school."

But it was not all "Happy Days."

West Tech also had a reputation as one of the toughest schools in the city. "Greasers" were king, the squeal of hot rods punctuated the air, and practically every day after school there was a fight in the nearby alleys. Yet teachers from those years—and many of them are still on staff—look back at it as the golden era or the good old days.

I talked with a music teacher at Lincoln Junior High School who taught at Tech when I was a student. Like all the teachers I spoke with about these times, his voice dripped with nostalgia.

"I missed maybe three days in my four years at Tech. Today that's unheard of, but that's the way it was back then. They used to teach self-discipline there. And a loyalty to the school. They made you feel you were something special."

"I had a study hall in the auditorium, maybe 200 kids, by myself and no trouble. A student helper took attendance for me and I could sit in the back and grade papers without any problems. God, chewing gum was a major offense back then. Look at how we have deteriorated, the verbal abuse we have to take, much less the physical."

How badly has West Tech deteriorated ? A quick comparison between 1967 and the present:

In 1967 daily attendance was around 95 percent. Two cuts a grading period dipped a student's grade one letter. Classes began at 8:30 a.m. and ended at 3:30 p.m. but the school remained open until 5 p.m. to accommodate the 26 clubs and athletic programs available to the students.

Most faculty club sponsors were not paid for their services—and often paid expenses out of their own pockets. The administration rewarded them with a late starting time.

Many friendships and romances were forged during after-school activities. Extra-curricular activities are a vital part of any education, revealing many hidden talents and kindling wide interests.

West Tech was a little society of its own. If the football team needed tickets, it went to the print shop. If the senior play needed costumes and scenery, it went to the sewing and art classes. If your car needed a tune-up, you brought it into the auto shop.

The atmosphere fostered cooperation and respect between students and faculty. Students monitored study halls, hallways and lunch rooms. We were the only students in the city allowed to go outside for lunch. Discipline consisted of swats, detentions, suspensions and eventually expulsion. Teachers knew they were backed up by an administration which contacted parents immediately.

The discipline was a legacy of 36-year principal Charles C. Tuck. A substitute who worked in the Cleveland system for 18 years told me he never met Tuck but heard about him from a great many teachers.

"Tuck was from the era when principals hired and fired," he said. "And he hired big, strong male teachers, ex-athletes who could knock around the kids if they stepped out of line."

What happened to Tuck's legacy?

His shadow began to disappear from the school in 1970 when West Tech became a neighborhood school, no longer drawing students from the entire West Side. With the advent of busing, many of its special classes, such as the college-level chemistry class, were dismantled.

"The federal court decided it was unfair to offer a course unless it was available in at least three schools," explained a former West Tech chemistry teacher who now teaches junior high math. Since the school system couldn't offer the chemistry course in at least three schools—it lacked the funds to offer more courses and qualified students to fill them

—the course was dropped. "Today," the former chemistry instructor adds, "they have trouble filling the few physics classes they have left."

Today's West Tech students can spend two years preparing for such jobs as salad maker, babysitter and short order cook—skills that can be learned in one week on the job.

"They made the students' goals way too low," a guidance counselor said.

The deterioration of the building, once a well-kept classic brick structure, matches its decline in instruction. Many glass doors are shattered, covered with plywood or plastic. The outdoor steps and indoor stairs are crumbling. Window shades are torn or missing. Paint is peeling everywhere. Many of the student's restrooms are closed because of vandalism. By the end of the day the halls are usually are filled with litter.

The sheer volume of class-cutting dwarfs anything attempted by previous generations. Attendance has dropped to between 70 and 75 percent, depending on the weather. And this does not include the large number of students that stream out the doors between periods.

As the day progresses, the classes become smaller and the hall traffic thins. "Many students just show up for a free breakfast and lunch," an English teacher said. "And no one cares if they leave," a teacher's aide said. "It makes it easier to teach the ones who want to learn.

"We stopped worrying about cutting when the administration put the job of enforcement on us," a veteran math teacher said. "If I called the parents of all the kids who cut, I'd be on the phone all night."

Two years ago, I met the previous principal walking around the building trying to combat truancy. "I'm not a principal anymore," he said. "I'm a policeman."

School spirit is practically non-existent and teacher morale is as low as that of the students. "My classes are pretty good this year but I can't believe that how far I've had to lower my standards," said a social studies teacher.

"Teachers used to stay here for 40 years, but not anymore," said a 25-year instructor. "The pressure is too much." Like most of the teachers I talked with, he plans to retire as soon as he puts in his required 30 years.

Extra-curricular activities have all but disappeared from the school. Classes start at 8:10 a.m., end at 2:30 p.m., and by 2:35 p.m. the halls are empty. There is no senior play, school orchestra and baseball team. The few clubs and sports teams that are available have trouble attracting participants.

The loss of out-of-class interaction has soured student-teacher relations. Cooperation has been replaced by mutual distrust. Even the coat closet, two feet from the principal's office, is kept locked.

The West Tech Tatler, once a free weekly paper read by almost everyone, today is a 25-cent monthly read by few. Front page stories on crime, vandalism and truancy read like a big-city daily.

Security guards, armed with expensive walkie-talkies, patrol halls once controlled by little old ladies sitting at desks. Study halls, where a student once could finish most of his homework, are as rare as detentions, mainly because there is little homework.

"You try to do what you can do in the classroom," an English teacher explained. "If you assign homework, the kids either say they lost it or they just don't do it."

"For the first time," said another, "I don't have enough textbooks for the students to take home."

To experience what West Tech was like in 1967, I sub at Lakewood High School. It also has a 9th grade class. If teachers must be absent, they often only take half the day off so their classes will not fall too far behind.

A senior assembly opens with a Pledge of Allegiance to the Flag. American flags hang from most classrooms. The experience reminds me of what is missing from West Tech today.

"You know what is wrong with this school?" asked a student who transferred to Tech from a small-town school system. "Too many kids won't accept any responsibility."

His comment struck a chord. I realized that when I was a student, West Tech taught not only the basics of reading, writing and math, but also imparted a sense of patriotism, responsibility, citizenship, discipline, punctuality and dependability.

These and all the other intangibles necessary to produce responsible citizens and competent employees are lacking at West Tech and most of other Cleveland public schools.

The only prescription for Cleveland's public school system is a good strong dose of old-fashioned West Tech discipline administered at all levels.

Perhaps surprisingly, the schools seemed to have reached a similar conclusion. Many junior highs are improved this year over recent years. A new school policy demands an automatic failure for a student with seven unexcused absences per grading period.

Yet there is still a long way to travel before standards abandoned somewhere along the road are restored. Teachers must once again be free to share their education with future generations in a relaxed atmosphere.

To begin this, the school system first must weed out the dangerous, over-age, professional students.

The West Tech student who threatened me with an iron bar, for example, had two typewritten pages of similar incidents in his file. An assistant principal told me, "We've had problems with him all year. But it seems like every time we try to take a kid like that out of school, they (downtown) are against us."

Teachers frequently express a conviction that the school board is more concerned with inflating attendance figures for funding purposes than protecting the teachers. Whether it is true or not, the teachers feel they have little support. Only the most violent incidents seem to bring action.

The students know it, take a suspension (vacation) and return heroes to their classmates. The teachers become more frustrated. A Cleveland substitute teacher with 18 years' experience expressed the feeling of most I met: "I used to love coming to school, now I hate it."

Another solution is a return of night school as a disciplinary tool. If the schools can afford a THINK program, which most English teachers consider useless, they can afford to establish a strong night school program. If the problem student really wants an education, let him come at night during his party time and at his own expense.

The system's new superintendent, Frederick Holliday, has stated that the solution to the school's financial woes is closing more schools. But this is merely an admission of defeat.

A more sensible goal would be to try to bring white students back into the system. As it is now, much of the city is paying for a school system that it does not use. There is a baby boom presently nearing school age. If Cleveland public schools were to improve dramatically, I believe enrollment would skyrocket—in turn attracting even greater state funding.

But before this can happen, someone from the school board or federal court is going to have to stand up and say out loud what thousands of Clevelanders already know. That school busing to achieve racial integration is a very expensive failure.

Like the war in Vietnam, it is a noble idea that has not lived up to its billing. Rather than achieving racial harmony and quality education for all, student busing has instead contributed to white flight, declining enrollment, school closings, teacher layoffs, inadequate instruction and fiscal problems.

Instead of harmony, I find today more racial animosity between students and faculty than existed 15 years ago. And until busing is ended, it is likely that many Clevelanders, particularly on the West Side, will continue to send their children to private schools and will continue to vote against increases in funding for public schools.

CHAPTER TWENTY-FIVE:
"Saying Farewell To West Tech"

—*Plain Dealer* Op-ed piece on September 13, 1995

FORGET THE ROCK and Roll Hall of Fame and Museum. Forget the Indians winning the World Series or the Browns capturing their first Super Bowl title.

Years from now historians will argue that the most significant local event of 1995 occurred on Aug. 30 when West Technical High School's doors failed to open for the first time in 84 years.

It sounded the death knell for the Cleveland public school system.

I believe this not just because I am a West Tech graduate. I believe this because I am also a Cleveland historian.

Only a generation ago West Tech was the crown jewel in one of the most respected and innovative urban school systems in the country.

Historians will point out that after World War II representatives from war-torn Germany and Japan visited West Tech to learn how best to reconstruct their ravaged educational systems.

They learned West Tech's lessons well. Germany's and Japan's economies flourished. Meanwhile our federal government dismantled West Tech while plunging our country into a trillion-dollar debt.

Today educators are traveling to Germany and Japan to copy their systems. The federal government should have left West Tech alone in the first place.

West Tech was a magnet school before anyone ever heard of a magnet school. Any high school student on Cleveland's West Side could attend

West Tech instead of their neighborhood school. (East Tech provided a similar opportunity for East Side students.)

Its draw was an unique curriculum that included courses like welding, machine shop, aircraft repair and carpentry. There was also a college prep major that emphasized science and math.

You want to talk busing? I took two buses for the privilege of attending West Tech. And the government didn't pay a penny of it. My parents had to squeeze the expense from their very tight budget.

West Tech was successful because its administration had the power to ship a troublemaker back to his or her neighborhood school. Thus, it could compete with non-public schools like St. Ignatius or St. Ed's. Either go along with the program or take a hike.

Yet we weren't a bunch of goodie-goodies. Far from it. West Tech was a tough inner-city school. We had gangs and we had fights.

But step through the doors of the huge four-story structure and it was a different story. It wasn't easy keeping discipline in the largest school in Ohio.

First, West Tech's principals had a tradition of hiring large male teachers, phys-ed types. Second, the teachers were allowed to run their classrooms with complete authority. They each had a wooden paddle hanging from their desks and they weren't afraid to use it. They'd show their technique their first couple days of school and the class would be peaceful the rest of the year.

It always amazes my classmates to recall that our toughest security guard was a middle-aged, 90-pound lady who sat at a desk in the first-floor hallway. No armed guards. No metal detectors. Her word was law because if she fingered you, the administration backed her to the limit.

The hallways were as quiet as the classrooms.

It wasn't a prison. We had a great time. There were enough extra curricular activities, clubs, sports and parties to make the day enjoyable.

Most pre-busing graduates will tell you that they loved West Tech.

What it had, and what is missing in Cleveland public schools today, was a safe, secure atmosphere that fostered education. Employers loved West Tech graduates. They stood in line to hire them before the ink was dry on their diplomas.

What happened? Very simply, federal judges who know nothing about education took over the school system and systematically destroyed it.

I visited West Tech the day its last class was due to graduate. About 100 of them. That's out of around 1,000 who had started there a few years earlier.

Daily attendance ran about 50 percent and even those numbers were inflated. (Compared with more than 90 percent in my era.)

The building was in disrepair. Except for some new boilers it looked as if there hadn't been a penny spent on maintenance over the last 20 years.

I don't blame the state for closing Tech. Most of us alumni see it as pulling the plug on a grand old lady suffering from an incurable disease. After all, our West Tech ceased to exist about two decades ago.

But what happened to West Tech borders on criminal neglect. If it was someone's child, the state would take custody. And that's just what it did.

It is probably too late to save Tech. As least as long as it is part of the Cleveland school system.

But I have one idea. Take West Tech, remodel it and turn it into a super school. Its basic structure is sound. It only needs new plumbing, electrical, windows, etc.

Return its power to throw people out, maybe to a dump-off school for losers, and it might flourish again.

Make it difficult to attend. Make the standards high. Instill pride. Watch it grow.

The system could probably close three or four other high schools and save tons of money.

A nice dream. But the Cleveland school system would never pull it off, even if it did save a fortune. Not while the federal courts control it. Not while all the lawyers and carpetbaggers have their fingers in the till.

You can elect all the L-teams or X-teams you want, but the school board has no real authority anymore. And the superintendent, whether appointed by the school board or the state, cannot make the necessary changes with a federal judge handcuffing him.

The only real solution to the Cleveland schools dilemma is to put the system out of business. Break it up.

The city of Cleveland has six police districts and six fire battalions. It needs six school districts. Each operating independently.

This would get the federal courts off our backs. Each would be the size of a large suburb like Parma. The schools would once again be manageable and responsive to the community.

Impossible, you say? I don't care what it takes. If necessary sell the administration building to pay for the reorganization. Break the city of Cleveland itself into six suburbs if you have to.

Just do it.

Every year, thousands of Cleveland public school students are being deprived of learning the basic skills needed for a free economy and a democratic country.

How long can we keep up this charade? If we don't do something soon, we'll all pay later.

Do it for West Tech.

CHAPTER TWENTY-SIX:
"CLEVELAND: Back Up And Start Over"

— a *Plain Dealer* Op-ed piece on January 9, 1996.

HAPPY BIRTHDAY, CLEVELAND. On New Year's Day our city began a yearlong celebration of its 200th birthday with a float in the Rose Parade.

What a great time for the grand old town. Thanks to the Cleveland Indians and the Rock and Roll Hall of Fame and Museum, we're sitting on top of the world, basking in newfound fame and glory. We should enjoy the recognition for as long as we can.

But as a Cleveland historian looking over the last 200 years with an eye to the future, I have a radical suggestion for the next century.

It's time to put the old thoroughbred of a city out to pasture. What a better time to call it quits than when you are on top of your game? Go out in a blaze of glory like another famous Clevelander, Jim Brown.

Because beneath the surface, under all the glitz, are a bunch of tired old neighborhoods struggling to survive.

Every election year I hear the same old refrain: "So what if downtown's booming, what are you doing about the neighborhoods?" It's usually spouted by a disgruntled councilman or wannabe mayoral candidate.

Yet there is a great cause for concern. For every neighborhood success story there are many more times problems.

Take your pick: Crime, drugs, pollution, decay, poverty, gangs, dysfunctional schools. They're all out of control and growing worse daily.

It's time for the city of Cleveland to admit to itself that the urban problems of modern America are just too big to solve.

Despite massive influxes of federal dollars over the past few decades the neighborhoods have deteriorated, not improved.

Cleveland should follow the lead of big business and the federal government. Downsizing is all the rage.

The city already has six police districts and six fire battalions. It should prepare for the 21st century by breaking itself up into six brand new independent suburbs.

The West Side would become Ohio City, Old Brooklyn and West Park. The new East Side would be called Cleveland, Glenville and Mt. Pleasant. Or pick your own names.

Sounds crazy? Maybe, let me explain.

What do all city of Cleveland residents have in common? They all want to move to the suburbs but can't afford to upgrade.

Why do they want to move? Two big reasons: Better schools and police protection. Safety is the big issue in the 1990s, in both the schools and the neighborhoods.

Why do the suburbs do a better job of providing services than the big city? They are more responsive because there aren't layers of bureaucrats between their leaders and their citizens.

And just as importantly, the suburbs aren't hampered by social engineers who live in Washington D.C. and think they know what's best for our nation's big cities, foisting experiments like school busing on them.

In one quick move, everyone in the city would now live in a suburb. The busing experiment would be over because it would no longer apply. Property values would immediately rise.

New school boards could actually promote education instead of stifling it. New local courts could back up the new police departments, administering justice swiftly, just as the U.S. Constitution requires.

It almost sounds too easy. Of course there would be some resistance from vested interests. But I think it would be an opportunity for everyone.

The mayor and city councilmen may be afraid of losing their jobs. But now there would be six mayors and six new councils. Who better to fill those positions that those with previous government experience?

Likewise with other city employees. I'm a city worker myself, a fire fighter. I'm sure there could be a provision to protect our jobs, giving us first priority in the new suburbs. Let the unions work out the details.

Some operations like the airport and water department may have to be taken over by the county. That's a bit tricky but not impossible.

It would force Cuyahoga County's government to make some long-overdue changes in its operation. It also needs a major overhaul. It has a $750 million budget overseen by three commissioners. It reminds me of a Latin American military junta.

In case you're not a student of Latin American politics, those countries south of the border don't operate very efficiently. You can't run a football team, a corporation or a government by committee.

No one is ultimately responsible for the big decisions, like the SAFE debacle.

The other major obstacle to overcome is what to do with downtown. Those big office buildings generate an awful lot of tax revenue and everyone would like a piece of the pie.

I'm sure there is a solution. Maybe let the county distribute it like the U.S. block grants. Maybe change the taxation system. Maybe attach it to the poorest neighborhoods to create a golden inner city.

What we need is a blue ribbon committee to work out the details. Give it a year to bring back a plan to voters.

Let's put Cleveland on the cutting edge of modern thought, like it was back in the glory days around the turn of the century. Let the nation watch in awe as we solve all our urban problems with one stroke of the pen.

It would be a birthday to remember.

CHAPTER TWENTY-SEVEN:
"A Poll Worker Has A Question: Why Can't We All Just Be Democrats?"

—Appeared in CoolCleveland.com on March 19, 2008.

I HAD THE rare opportunity to work as a precinct poll worker in the recent historic primary election. My job was to pass out ballots to Democrats, Republicans and Independents. I shared a table in a suburban middle school with a number of other poll workers. We pulled a 16-hour stint during a raging snowstorm. It was during a lull before the storm that the idea struck me like a bolt of lightning: What if everyone in Cuyahoga County voted as a Democrat?

In my opinion, the Republican voters were basically wasting their efforts, backing candidates in the primary election that have little chance of winning in November. There already seemed to be a trend in that direction. The day after the primary, The *Plain Dealer* reported that 16,000 Cuyahoga County Republicans had jumped ship and voted on the Democratic ballot. We saw some of that action at our table but paid it little heed. Yet the old switcheroo put our local Democratic Party leaders in an uproar. They claimed that the Republicans crossed party lines only to influence whether Hillary Clinton or Barack Obama would face Republican Presidential candidate John McCain in November.

I thought they should have welcomed the new Democrats with open arms. That is what County Democratic Chairman Jimmy Dimora did when three Republican Mayors switched parties on Election Day. He was quoted as saying that they were just coming over to the winning team.

Maybe that is what the 16,000 Republican voters were doing. Maybe they are on the cutting edge of a wholesale conversion. For all practical purposes Cuyahoga County has been under one party rule for as long as most of us can remember.

Who can blame the local Republicans for wanting to add their two cents to the 10th district Congressional election? It features the world famous Dennis Kucinich, the hottest race in town.

It was amazing comparing the Republican and Democratic ballots that I was handing out. The Democratic ballot was so much longer. There were so many names, so many choices, so many incumbents. The Republicans were lucky if they could find even one candidate per office to be led to the slaughter.

I suddenly realized that Cuyahoga County's Republicans had been wasting their primary votes for all these years. A Democrat could vote for Dennis Kucinich twice on the same ballot, once for President and once for Congressman. Why couldn't Republicans have that kind of fun? I envisioned the day when Kucinich would also run for County Commissioner and Common Pleas Judge. Then he would be guaranteed at least one job on the public payroll no matter how low his ratings sank.

In the spirit of Barack Obama, I say it is time for a wholesale change in the way we handle elections in Cuyahoga County. What if every Republican followed this new trend, crossing over and becoming a Democrat? Then the voting would become really interesting.

Everyone knows that if you want to be elected to a public office in Cuyahoga County you must fulfill two important requirements. First, you must have the blessing of the Democratic Party. Second, you must have an Irish surname, especially if you are running for one of the many judicial slots. That is, unless your last name is Russo. I counted four Russo's out of 28 candidates recommended on the County Democratic Party's official sample ballot.

In fact, I was amazed at how many voters took the Democrats' sample ballot into the election booth with them. They were all just voting the straight party ticket. It reminded me of the elections the Soviet Union conducted during the Cold War. Everyone could vote as long as you voted for the Communist Party's candidates. Cuyahoga County's one party system already closely resembles the former Soviet Union's. Once all the Republican voters cross over the transition will be complete.

Of course, life in Communist Russia was no bed of roses but what the heck, living in Cuyahoga County is not much fun anymore, either. If current trends continue we will soon have more citizens collecting welfare than taxpayers paying for it. It was only a few decades ago that Cuyahoga County was one of the largest and most prosperous counties in the nation. It would be too easy to blame our current Democratic Party leaders for its steep decline.

Once we all become Democrats we can jump on the bandwagon and blame the President of The United States for all our problems. That is also what the Soviet Union did.

ABOUT THE AUTHOR

PETER JEDICK's career as a best-selling author and historian spans several decades. On a national scale, he has authored four books and written for several magazines including *America in World War II* and *Baseball America*. As a local writer in Northeast Ohio, he has written for every major news organization including the Cleveland *Plain Dealer*, *Cleveland Magazine*, *Sun Newspapers* and *The Cleveland Press*.

As the recipient of an Excellence in Journalism award from the Press Club of Cleveland, Jedick has been interviewed and recognized by numerous TV and radio shows. He also had a stint as an award-winning radio commentator for WKSU-FM, an NPR (National Public Radio) station.

Jedick is best known for his novel *HIPPIES* (Amazon), a fictional account of campus life surrounding the tragic events of the 1970 Kent State shootings. (www.hippiesbook.com) *HIPPIES* was well received on college campuses across the country. He graduated cum laude, with outstanding honors from Kent State University in 1971.

Jedick's second novel, *The West Tech Terrorist* (Amazon), is a fictional account of life in Cleveland when the U.S. was at the brink of World War II and Eliot Ness was Cleveland's Safety Director. (www.westtechterrorist.com) In this book, Jedick takes us on an adventure as Ness and his student sidekick team up to foil a plot hatched by Nazi sympathizers. He takes us back in time while perfectly capturing the mood of the city—and the country—in that era.

Another popular book, *CLEVELAND: Where the East Coast Meets the Midwest*, is an historic account of stories about his fair city, once referred to as the "Best Location in the Nation," and includes its challenges and triumphs from Eliot Ness to Millionaire's Row and everything in between.

Jedick's first book was *League Park*, a book detailing the early days of Cleveland history and its first professional baseball stadium.